WITHDRAWN
University of
Illinois Library
at Urbana-Champaign

JOURNEYS ALONG THE MATRIX

JOURNEYS ALONG THE MATRIX

three plays
by
Martha Boesing

Leslie Bowman, *Artist*

VANILLA PRESS
Minneapolis

Copyright © 1978 Martha Boesing

First printing.

All rights reserved. No part of this book may be reproduced, transmitted, or performed for any reason, by any means, without permission in writing from the author.

Music has been composed for all of these plays and is available upon request. (*The Gelding* and *Love Song for an Amazon*, music by Paul Boesing. *River Journal*, music by John Franzen.)

Library of Congress Catalog Card No.: 77-88048

Boesing, Martha
   Journeys Along the Matrix.

Minneapolis, MN.: Vanilla Press
96 p.

ISBN 0-917266-15-3

Printed in the United States of America

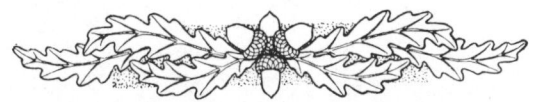

For the women At the Foot of the Mountain:
Phyllis, Jan, Robyn, Aurora, and Cecilia,
and for Paul.

CONTENTS

Introduction	7
The Gelding	13
River Journal	31
Love Song for an Amazon	81

INTRODUCTION

I met Martha Boesing in the Minneapolis airport. I was coming to town to see the October rehearsals of her production of *River Journal* (1975). "How will I know you?" "Well," she decided, "I'm very tall. *Quite* tall, and I'll be wearing my boots and jeans. And I'll have a flower in my mouth." As it turned out, she was wearing a very long skirt (and boots, though I couldn't see them). Determined to find boots and jeans on very long legs, however, I began to panic staring at feet — until I heard a muffled, teeth-clenched version of my name and turned to see a bespectacled woman with a marigold in her mouth. She wasn't *that* tall.

Martha grew up in New Hampshire, living with her mother. She wrote her first play while studying at Connecticut College for Women. After an apprenticeship in summer stock companies as well as in school and college theaters, an M.A. in English literature, and postgraduate work in theater, she cofounded and codirected The Moppet Players, now The Children's Theater of Minneapolis. Later she joined the core company of The Firehouse Theater as an actor, fund-raiser, and closet playwright (1965-68). It was here she met actor and composer Paul Boesing who was to become her husband and partner for many years. Through such diverse commissions as creating plays and operas for the Minnesota Opera Company, for the American Friends Service Committee — under whose auspices she and Paul created and traveled with Earth Family, a theater commune — and for the Academy Theater in Atlanta, Martha maintained her radical vision of politics and aesthetics. In 1974, with four other actors, Martha and Paul moved to Minneapolis to found At the Foot of the Mountain. This company's first productions were *Pimp* and *The Gelding*. The second production — produced by Martha and Jan Magrane, the only two surviving members of the theater's first generation — was *River Journal*.

During this ongoing theater life, Martha married twice. She is the mother of three children (Curtis, Rachel, and Jennifer) with whom she and I now live in a small blue house, across from a park, in Minneapolis' inner city. We're trying to find ways to make life in the house connect directly with life in the theater — or, more importantly, we're trying to connect life in the theater with life in the house.

If politics may be broadly defined as "the way we are with each other," then anything that affects how we connect with each other is political. The premise of Martha Boesing's plays is that feelings are the source of our connection, and her plays are plays of connection and wholeness. They have connected me with myself, the theater, and other living beings: They have validated my deepest woman self by helping me know that I know; they have shaken me and moved me to a new bonding with other women; they have renewed my conviction that the theater is a place of fantasy, vision, and truth. In a world where "man" has lost touch with "his" feelings — thus destroying the earth and its peoples — each of these connections is revolutionary and a cause for celebration. This introduction is a celebration of Martha Boesing's plays.

Her plays are deeply political. The double source of their strength lies in her skill, as a person who has lived for twenty-five years in the theater, and in her courage, as one who has lived for forty-one years as a woman. It is an act of personal courage for Martha to lay bare her own feelings, to experience, examine, and to respect them. It is an act of artistic courage to make plays that not only are feeling experiences but that also call on feelings as the source of vision and a basis of political action. These three plays are this new kind of play: *The Gelding*, about men's struggles with patriarchal values; *River Journal*, about a woman's struggle to disentangle herself from these values; and *Love Song for an Amazon*, about matriarchy and the rediscovery of women's values.

When I first read *The Gelding*, my heart raced, for I knew I wasn't just seeing characters talk about their problems, I was experiencing these problems: I was a witness, from the inside, to how the patriarchy turned onto a course of self-destruction. This witnessing was possible because of the structure of the piece: layers, a series of scenes intuitively connected by feelings rather then linearly connected by logic or time. Martha was expressing a vision of the root of experience not in words but in happenings. The key is in what *happens*, as in all good theater.

Pimp, a three-woman companion piece to *The Gelding* (see list of plays by Martha Boesing at the back of the book), works in similar ways to dramatize how women have sold each other out to and for the men in their lives. Again the structure is not linear, but layered and cumulative, and the characters created with love and respect. "Oh yes," I realized as I read, "I have done this. I have felt this. This play is about me. Someone has seen me. I am part of the world." If we can see, we can change. That is the connection and the hope.

River Journal — a modern morality play about Everywoman, and an epic of sorts — does move in the linear path of Ann's painful journey away from marriage and a male-identified world to separation and a woman-identified point of view. But the journey is so embellished, textured, stopped, started, haunted with myths (Snake), masks (Vera, Carla, Mom), poetry (the Songs), and fantasies (the Journal), that I feel as if I've danced every dimension of Ann's quest. As I read *River Journal*, I was moved by the extravagant theatricality of it — Snake, the nightmares, the ax, and the altar, Mom, and the masks — all of it. As I lived with the play, I changed my life because of it. In a nonanalytical way, *River Journal* crystallized for me the lesson of experience: that women and men habitually relate heirarchically. In the company of men, women traditionally metamorphose into either "Vera" — the coquette, seductress, the little girl — or "Carla" — the accomodater, the taker-care-of, the Mom. Both masks require that we define our individual behavior in terms of vertical power, and both masks are as old as the patriarchy. None of us is free.

"Carla" was the mask I wore most often. She fit me better, but I kept my "Vera" around just in case. Here I was chairing the directing program in the theater department of a large university, and I caught myself daily, hourly, wearing these masks. How did I negotiate for a change in our production schedule so that I might direct a new feminist script called *River Journal*? I played "Carla" and "Vera" depending on which mask proved most persuasive. I was appalled at the recognition. Then incredulous. Then delighted. Finally, to understand the game! Finally, to understand what my choices were! After directing *River Journal*, I chose to quit my job. It seemed hypocritical to spend energy trying to avoid the traps of these masks when I could participate in their destruction. I moved to Minneapolis to work At the Foot of the Mountain and helped transform it into the feminist theater collective it is now — passionate, struggling, angry, joyous, questioning.

In April of 1976, a few months after At the Foot of the Mountain became a women's ensemble, Martha wrote *Love Song for an Amazon*. In sunburst scenes that are light, affectionate, and celebratory, the whole history of our relations with each other — past, present, and future — happens. The whole history of our struggle to survive men's values (and rediscover our own) happens. I smile at the weight of these words I write in response to a "song."

Balancing her work as a playwright and child-guardian, Martha Boesing is also an actor, director, and administrator At the Foot of the Mountain where — through the performance of Martha's plays (and "songs"), through the performance of scripts by other women, and through community events and rituals — we work *collectively* asking such questions as : How can we connect theater with life? What is the correlation between the choices we make as performers and the choices we make as persons? How can theater work as a spiritual and healing force in our community? How can theater best serve radical political change? How can we stop giving in to a system in which power over others is the common standard for success? How does a women's theater differ from the theater of our heritage (theater written and produced by men)?

Our work is an ongoing process of developing our company voice and radicalizing our collective vision. As Martha does in her plays, we strive to create theater that is informed by consciousness rather than rhetoric, to move audiences rather than to chastise them, and to be as committed to understanding the theater as we are to understanding human liberation. We search for new ways to act, to direct, and to write while training ourselves to understand: Process is *always* as important as product. As our experience of acting, directing, and writing diverges more and more from the traditions we have been taught, we search for new words and forms. As Martha wrote in her description of the women At the Foot of the Mountain,

> We struggle to relinquish such traditions as linear plays, proscenium theater, nonparticipatory ritual, and seek to reveal theater that is circular, intuitive, personal, involving. As witnesses to the destructiveness of a society which is alienated from itself, we are a theater of protest. As participants in the prophecy of a new world which is emerging through the rebirth of women's consciousness, we are a theater of celebration.

Martha Boesing's plays are rituals of celebration, radical visions of how we can move toward connection and wholeness. They are political and holy, humane and angry. They return theater and myth to women. They nourish our souls.

— Phyllis Jane Wagner

The Gelding

THE CHARACTERS

EBAN, *the Father*
JULES, *the Son*
BEETHOVEN, *a Mute*

Beethoven is an adjunct of Eban. He plays an instrument, preferably a horn. He improvises throughout the play between or under or in the midst of the dialog. Eban keeps him in a cardboard box.

INTRODUCTION

In May, 1974, the Atlanta *Constitution* reported that

> A Harris County grand jury has indicted a petroleum engineer on charges he attempted to murder his 13-year-old son by exposing him to radioactive material while he slept. The indictment accused Crocker, 43, of committing assault to murder, castration, assault to maim, disfiguring and injury to a child . . . "I love my children," Crocker said.

The Gelding is a patriarchal ritual. It can be staged in any competitive arena — such as a boxing ring, a court of law, a race track, a duelling ground. Each scene should be entered into the way one enters rounds in a sports event. It should be played out ritualistically, making note of the winner of each round. The events must not be hurried. The stakes are life and death, and the dance between the three players is a slow one.

Scene 1

The three actors come on stage.
They sing directly to the audience in a round.

ALL 3:   Oh, Absalom, my son, my son.
             Oh, Absalom, my son, my son.
             Would to God I had died for thee, my son.
             Would to God I had died for thee, my son.
             Oh, Absalom, my son, my son.
             Oh, Absalom, my son, my son.

Scene 2

EBAN *sits.* BEETHOVEN *is in his cardboard box beside* EBAN. JULES *enters.*

EBAN: Son, I'd like a word . . . .

    JULES *approaches. He looks at* EBAN.

EBAN: How are things?

    JULES *extends his hand, palm up.* EBAN *slaps it in greeting.*

EBAN: Time for a man to man . . . .

    JULES *slaps* EBAN *across the face.*

EBAN: Trouble, Jules?

    No response from JULES.

EBAN: Problems?

    No response from JULES.

EBAN: We should talk more, you and I . . . .

> JULES *very slowly raises his extended middle finger to* EBAN'S *mouth.*
> EBAN *looks at* JULES. *He opens his mouth.*
> EBAN *first sucks and then bites* JULES' *finger.*
> *Blood gushes out of* JULES' *mouth.*

Scene 3

EBAN *takes* BEETHOVEN *out of his box. He gets in the box.*
BEETHOVEN *plays.*
JULES *enters. He pulls* EBAN *out of the box.*

JULES: Hey, Dad! Hey, Jelly Roll! Hear how I cleaned out the Corral last night? Turned it out, Dad, really turned it out! Yeh! I was sitting around, feeling shitty, jacking off, felt like I needed some action. So I got on my bike and took off. Clipping down the road, hauling ass, man, I was flying! Got to the Corral and went inside. Filled with rednecks it was. Got myself a beer and sat down beside this fatass old redneck, who was laughing it up with his girl. She was all knockers, all right out there, big old fat cow. I said, "Hey, wanna move that hunk of flesh off my part of the bar?" She looks at her redneck friend and I could tell he was pissed. I figured I'd go him some. So I say to her: "Hey! What's your name?" Well, she didn't answer, just poked old redneck and took off for the powder room. He was getting all hot under the collar and he looked at me and I said, "Man, your woman looks unfit for the pig farm!" "Look, motherfucker! You cut that out or I'll slap you under this bar!" he snaps back. So BOOM! I lopped him one. Right there in the bar. Then I see all his redneck friends come up behind him and man I gulp my beer and go peeling out the back door. I can hear them all coming after me, all the old Ford pickups . . . brockkkkk, brockkkkk. I got on my bike and peeled outta there! Man, those sonofabitches are so pussy-whipped they couldn't begin to catch up with me. Dumb rednecks — they all think they got big cocks!

JULES *leaves.*
BEETHOVEN *holds* EBAN *in his arms and rocks him.*

Scene 4

JULES *enters.* EBAN *speaks from* BEETHOVEN's *lap.*

EBAN: You're late.

Silence.

EBAN: Where you been?
JULES: Swimming.
EBAN: Where?
JULES: Swimming hole.
EBAN: Who with?
JULES: The guys.
EBAN: What guys?
JULES: The guys down at school.
EBAN: Your mother and I don't approve of them, you know.
JULES: I know.
EBAN: I thought you didn't like them.
JULES: I don't.
EBAN: Why go swimming then?
JULES: I like to swim.

EBAN *gets up and approaches* JULES.
He takes his son over his knee and spanks him.

JULES *leaves.*

EBAN *puts* BEETHOVEN *in his box.* EBAN *leaves.*

Scene 5

BEETHOVEN *plays in his box.*
JULES *comes out and begins to dance, slow and easy.*
EBAN *comes out. Looks. Slowly joins the dance.*
They don't touch, don't make contact, but they are clearly dancing with each other. The dance is very sexual.

JULES (*after a while, still dancing*): What's in the box, Dad?
EBAN: Nothing.
JULES: Something.
EBAN: Nothing concerns you.
JULES: I'd like to know, though.
EBAN: I'm telling you — it's none of your business, Jules. It's my business and no one else's.
JULES: I heard an old priest once who said secrets were the most terrible thing we got inside us.
EBAN: Priests! Women! Children! You're all alike! Pry, pry, pry! Always wanting to know things. About me. About everybody. Saying secrets are bad. Well, that's bullshit, son. Some things no one can take away from him and no one can possess — not even God. If you didn't have something which is all yours, at your very center, some special place, that no one can ever get into, why then you'd be just like everybody else — and that's nobody. Nobody! You'd just wash away like the rain on dry, flat land. You'd be dead, son. Dead!
JULES: OK, Dad.

JULES *leaves.*

EBAN *takes* BEETHOVEN *out of his box and talks to him.*

EBAN: It's all a mystery to me, Beethoven.

BEETHOVEN *plays.*

EBAN: Nothing makes sense.

BEETHOVEN *plays.*

EBAN: Just goes on going . . . round, round, round . . . .

BEETHOVEN *plays.*

EBAN: Yep! It's all a mystery to me.

Scene 6

JULES *enters.* EBAN *puts* BEETHOVEN *back in his box.*

JULES: Dad?

No response.

JULES: Dad, I was wondering . . . .
EBAN: Your mother said you forgot to feed the dog.
JULES: Dad, I'd like to . . . .
EBAN: Your mother said you didn't make your bed.
JULES: There's a game this afternoon . . . we could . . . .
EBAN: Your mother said you got in late last night.
JULES: Are you going hunting this weekend?
EBAN: Jules, it's time for you to grow up.
JULES: Are you?
EBAN: It's time for you to become a man, . . .
JULES: Dad?
EBAN: be responsible, . . .
JULES: Dad?
EBAN: take care of yourself, . . .
JULES: Dad, are you going hunting?
EBAN: stop the whining.
JULES: What about the game, Dad?
EBAN: Are you listening to me?
JULES: Or hunting?
EBAN: Hunting?!

EBAN *leaves.*

JULES: I was walkin' out in the woods, Dad, with my friends, and we came to this turn in the path, and one of the guys said, "This is the way," and I said, "Nope, that's the wrong way; this is the way." But they went their way anyway. And so I went mine. After a while the brush got thick, but I kept on pushing through it. It got thicker and thicker, but I kept on going my way. And then I turned around and the path I had just been walkin' on was gone! I was lost, Dad!

Pause.

I was hopin' you'd find me.

JULES *leaves.*

Scene 7

EBAN *enters. He takes* BEETHOVEN *out of his box and is discovered by* JULES.

EBAN: You want something?

JULES: Yes, Sir.

EBAN: You want to become something?

JULES: Yes, Sir. I do, Sir.

EBAN: What makes you think you are qualified?

No response.

EBAN: Can you pay your bills, empty the garbage, fix the plumbing, mow the lawn, spank the children, screw your wife, unscrew bottle tops, build houses, drive trucks, work at the bank, tip the waitress, shoot a gun, dig holes, swim the channel, ride motorcycles, choose the wine, play pool, handle a switchblade, win at the races, drink gin, kill soldiers, smoke cigars, sit at a desk from nine till five, turn off, and keep from crying?

JULES: Oh, yes, Sir. Yes, Sir. Of course, Sir.

Pause. They stare at each other.

EBAN: Do you think you're gonna live forever?

EBAN *leaves.* JULES *stares down at* BEETHOVEN *who plays his horn.*

Scene 8

EBAN *enters with an egg. He tosses it to* JULES. *They play with it, sparring with each other.*

JULES: I just black out, Dad. I just black out.

Pause.

This one was a real ringer. She was a number nine knock-out! Tight little ass, pretty tits — no bra on — I could tell. Long brown legs, mmmmm . . . I nabbed her right out on the corner of the street. My blood was pounding, like I was going crazy. I mean I didn't decide to rape her! She was just calling right out to me with her eyes and her tits, you know, and her mouth that was all soft and wet. "Come here, boy! Come over here, boy!" I grabbed her arm and pulled her down the alley. It was five o'clock in the afternoon and the busiest street in the city! And the traffic was rushing by, screeching and honking — cars, buses, trucks, people — all moving and pushing up against each other. Beep! Beep! Broom! Broom! I threw her down in the alley, and I tore off her skirt, and I pulled down her panties. Oh, man! There it was, just waiting for me — dark and slippery and warm. I could hardly stand it! I was dancing all around her, pulling my pants down, sticking my tongue in and out and in and out. Whew! She was something else. She was a knock-out, Dad! Course she was screaming and kicking, but nobody was paying any attention. All the noise from the cars covered it up, you know — the trucks honking their horns. Beep! Beep! Broom! Broom! Honking and honking at each other. Broom! Bee-ep! Bee-ep! Brooo-oomm! Brooo-oomm!

Pause.

Then I blacked out.
EBAN: You blacked out?
JULES: I always do.
EBAN (*shaking him*): Jules! What do you mean you blacked out?
JULES: I don't remember, Dad. I don't remember anything.

Pause.

Next thing I knew, I was down at the police station.
EBAN: The police got you?
JULES: Yeh. (EBAN *is shocked.*) It's OK, Dad. They let me off. It was my first offense. They let me off.

EBAN *holds up the egg. He gives a knife to* JULES *who slowly and cruelly bores a hole in the egg with it.* EBAN *catches the egg fluid and wipes it on* JULES' *face.*

JULES *blacks out.*

EBAN *approaches him, leans over him, reaches to touch him, almost touches him, and doesn't.*

EBAN *puts* BEETHOVEN *back in his box and leaves.*

SCENE 9

JULES (*coming to*): Eban! Eban! (EBAN *enters.* BEETHOVEN *slowly comes out of his box by himself. They enact the dream as* JULES *tells it.*) I was dreaming. I was walking up this river. I was walking up, pushing against the current. Pushing back the water. Muddy ... muddy ... It got muddier as I went. There were crocodiles in the water and their mouths were huge — open, wide. And snakes were hanging down from the branches over my head. I fought them off with my knife. The light kept fading and I couldn't see. And I kept pushing back the water — it got thicker and thicker. I began to panic. Then I saw this figure on the bank. I could hardly make him out, but I pulled myself over to the bank to get a better look. He was filthy! He was wearing old torn rags, covered with dried blood. His face was scarred and hideous. I pulled myself up onto the bank and I grabbed at his feet. I opened my mouth and the words that fell out were: "Where's the moon, father?" (*He laughs.*) He just sat there without saying anything, looking down at me curiously. Then suddenly he threw back his head and he started singing.

EBAN (*sings, in a loud, cracking voice, like a Country Western star*):
>In my day I have met ten thousand souls.
>I have walked across this land from hole to hole.
>I know all there is to know throughout the land,
>And I'm offerin' you
>This helpin' hand.
>
>I've seen murderers and heroes come and go.
>Ain't no man can be trusted with the dough.
>Everything you see is as shiftin' as the sand,
>So I'm offerin' you
>This helpin' hand.
>
>Ain't no one's ever learned to stop the war.
>There ain't no way to keep from feelin' poor.
>It's all a pack o' lies; so do you understand
>The only thing worth shit's
>This helpin' hand.

JULES (*sings, like a Rock star; it is a contest*):
>Absalom, son of the king
>Was born into sorrow and grief,
>The people of Israel gave him their hearts

And he stole their hearts, like a thief.

>Absalom!
>Absalom!
>Take up your enemy's sword!
>It's the war of mankind you are fighting,
>With the heart-rending cry of the Lord!

The king and his son disagreed.
They got into a terrible fight.
The king turned away, and his servants proclaimed:
"We will bring back your people tonight."

All over the face of the land,
The men joined Absalom's fight.
"I am young, I am strong, my father!" he cried.
"I'll defeat you in battle tonight!"

>Absalom!
>Absalom!
>Take up your enemy's sword!
>It's the war of mankind you are fighting
>With the heart-rending cry of the Lord!

But as Absalom raced toward the throne
To prove to his father his worth,
His head became fixed in the limbs of a tree,
And he hung between heaven and earth.

The servants of David took spears
And drove them through Absalom's heart.
And they came with the news to the throne of the king,
saying, "Now we are no more apart."

King David went up to his room,
And he threw back his head, and he cried:
"Absalom, Absalom, my son, my son
Would to God it was me who had died!"

>Absalom!
>Absalom!
>Take up your enemy's sword!
>It's the war of mankind you are fighting
>With the heart-rending cry of the Lord!

BEETHOVEN *beats himself with the knife. He beats relentlessly.*

EBAN *and* JULES *move in very slowly.* EBAN *shuts* BEETHOVEN *up in the box.*

Scene 10

JULES *paints* EBAN'S *face in white makeup, with large, sad, black eyes. He places* EBAN *high up on a chair or a platform.*

JULES *moves around* EBAN *in a primitive dance, using the knife as a rhythm stick. The dance ends with* JULES *destroying* BEETHOVEN'S *box.*

Meanwhile, BEETHOVEN *escapes to a distant corner. He tolls a bell and/or plays very slow music on his horn.*

JULES *and* BEETHOVEN *are creating a duet: two acolytes at* EBAN'S *altar.*

Scene 11

EBAN (*from his chair or platform*): Boy! You ain't seen nothin'! You — my son, Jules — you — are a green twig, a stupid fink! You think you have to learn everything for yourself. You won't take no learning from ones who know. Stupid! I know. I been there. I been everywhere. There ain't no flesh I ain't smelled and licked. There ain't no hole on God's earth I ain't stuck my dick into. I could teach you some things!

There was this old lady. Old, fat lady. Name of Maud. She ran a house where I grew up. She thought she knew everything there was to know. Maybe she did — sitting out in front of her house, watching the boys go in and out, in and out. Her eyes was mean, slanty and mean! Her hands —

big as a gorilla's! She never did no harm, but she looked like she could kill. I went there when I was a boy. Everybody in town went there. There wasn't no choice in the matter. Maud put me with a girl who was thirteen. Thirteen — hardly started bleedin'! But that girl knew every trick in the trade. I went upstairs with her, snortin' like a bull. I pulled my pants off quick as lightnin' and jumped on top of her like I seen it done in the movies. But I couldn't do it. I couldn't get it up! She was real sweet to me, too, real easy! But all her tricks weren't no use. I could tell she thought I was real dumb. I lay beside her with my pants down, shakin' every time she touched me. I was softer than a girl! I left there ashamed; and I've never forgiven her for that. There ain't no shame in the world like that. Maud eyed me going out the door. She knew. And I hated her. Ten years later I came back there. I grabbed old fat Maud and took her up to that same room with the flowered wallpaper, same old bare light bulb hanging from the ceiling. And I tore her clothes off her, and I fucked her in every hole in her fat body! In and out, in and out! Waiting for her to scream. Nothing. So I beat her with a stick. I beat the shit out of her. And I screamed at her: Whore! Cunt! You lick the asses of the universe! You suck! You shove shit up your cunt for us to eat! You breed murderers! Every pisser in this world is your child! Every vile deed in the universe is yours! You are the mother of all my sins! You are a MOTHER! I was sweatin' . . . black slimy sweat, and my skin was burning like I was a witch tied to a stake and my prick was sorer than a sow's tit. There was nothing left in me. She had taken it all. I was done. She put her clothes on and went downstairs. Not a word. Not a sound.

Pause.

She had me beat.

EBAN *leaves.*

Scene 12

BEETHOVEN *hangs* JULES *up high, upside down by his feet.*

EBAN *enters.*
He kisses BEETHOVEN *on the mouth.*
He kisses JULES *on the mouth.*
Gently he rubs the knife in and out between the boy's thighs.

EBAN (*like a nurse, taking care of a diaper rash on an infant*): Sssssshhhh . . . there, there, don't be scared . . . it won't hurt . . . soon it'll be over . . . hush now . . . hush-a-bye . . . that's my baby . . . easy now . . . nothin' to be scared of . . . I won't let anyone hurt my baby . . . easy now, easy . . . let it go . . . nothin's gonna happen bad . . . no one will hurt you . . . that's a boy . . . soon it'll all be over . . . soon everythin'll be fine . . . hush-a-bye . . . that's my baby . . . such a good boy . . . such a beautiful baby . . . you're gonna be fine . . . just fine.

BEETHOVEN *plays a lullaby.* EBAN *leaves.*

Scene 13

BEETHOVEN *takes* JULES *down very slowly. He places him tenderly in a wheel chair. A crude thing, backless, perhaps, old casters on a stool or handbuilt wooden structure.*

EBAN *enters.* JULES *is sitting apart, in his wheel chair, hardly conscious.*

EBAN: Beethoven . . . Beethoven, . . . you there?

BEETHOVEN *plays his horn.*

EBAN: You saw him, Beethoven. You saw what was happening . . . . (*Pause.*) Didn't you?

BEETHOVEN *plays.*

EBAN: All those years he was growing up . . . I was — scared of him in a way. I remember the first time I held him, when she brought him home from the hospital. I thought he would break. He seemed . . . wonderful somehow. I

27

didn't want him to turn out like that. He was a beautiful baby, Beethoven. But he changed. He changed — like the day changes into the night. He became rough. Mean. Like the rest. He never liked women much. It always made me kind of sad. Sometimes he reminded me of a woman — soft. He was always reaching out — like wind. I did it for him, Beethoven. Did I do wrong?

EBAN *weeps. He takes* JULES *in his arms, rocking him like a baby.*

EBAN (*sings*):

>Oh, Absalom, my son, my son.
>Oh, Absalom, my son, my son.
>Would to God I had died for thee, my son.
>Would to God I had died for thee, my son.
>Oh, Absalom, my son, my son.
>Oh, Absalom, my son, my son.

EBAN *exits, carrying* JULES *in his arms.*

BEETHOVEN *plays.*

The End

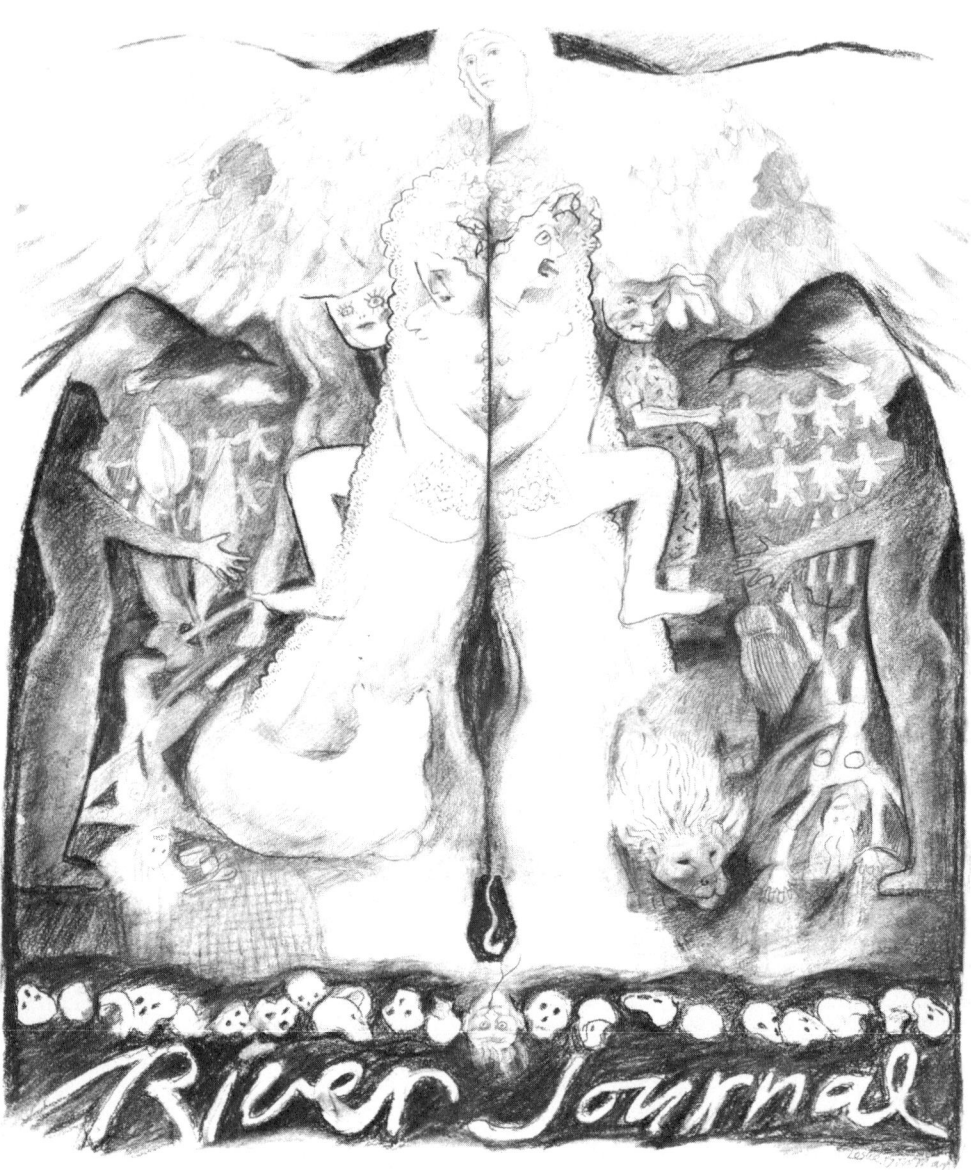

River Journal

AUTHOR'S NOTES

We act out our society's systems of belief with certain ritualistic behavior patterns that have become so ingrained in our daily living that we do not even notice them. *River Journal* deals with the ritual patterns of marriage in a male-dominated society in which ownership is power.

I discovered the particular patterns of this ritual by examining my own behavior inside of two marriages, both with very kind and gentle men who struggled as my allies — valiantly, but unsuccessfully — to break these patterns. I found that, because power in my society is defined in terms of our relationships to others rather than to ourselves (one above, one below, beginning with the way we experience our sexuality), I always related to the men in my marriages as if I were either the flirtatious and obsequious underling (Vera) who maintained her security by flattery and seduction, or as if I were the caretaker overseer (Carla) who maintained her security by smoothing over any trouble spots in the household and by creating an irresistible, comfortable nest for her mate. I began to observe that, in subtle and not-so-subtle ways, I came out of either a Vera space or a Carla space to every man in my life: the men I worked with, the man who fixed my car, even the postman. It was a horrifying discovery — until I realized that every woman in my society does the same. We all play Vera and Carla to the men in our lives. It is a given of our society, an inevitable behavior pattern nurtured by the system. It is a ritual that needs to be brought to light, examined, and finally changed, destroyed, so that a new ritual can be born from the ashes.

River Journal is not a play about an individual woman — an Ann, or a Martha. It is an enactment of an ongoing, daily ritual which we have so integrated into our lives that we take it for granted. The play should not, therefore, be presented naturalistically, despite the "realistic" dialog of some of the scenes. All of the scenes are economically condensed to their ritual center, down to the bone marrow, which is their common denominator. In rehearsal, I found it useful to have the actors fill the scenes out improvisationally, and slowly pare them down to the center again, in order to claim their own individual experiences within the lines.

River Journal is a myth of feminine consciousness. It should unfold before us, not with artfulness — because sophisticated art traditionally asks that we bring our minds and our reason to witness its unfolding — but with a childlike ingenuousness — because judgment is not appropriate in the presence of our childhood rituals. What is asked for is participation and an open heart. The actors should come to the script as children, because the ritual of marriage in our society is childlike in its naivety and innocence. The injuries perpetuated by this corrupt institution and its insane rituals are not caused by evil or malicious people but by ignorant people who have a childish, blind faith in the customs of their parent society. The feelings given off by the theatrical setting seen upon entering the performing space will let the audience know immediately what is expected of them, and they, too, will perhaps become as children.

And *River Journal* is itself a ritual. Like all rituals, in order to be meaningful, it must not be only larger than life, but it must also be filled with an utterly immediate and real life of its own. If the play is held up as a mask (the front face of this ritual) then the actors will discover an enormous lattitude to bring themselves and their own stories to this event. It will become your ritual and the ritual of your community in a deeply personal way, as rightly it should.

The set and costume suggestions I have made for *River Journal* befit the idea of a ritual and spring from the only rituals that have had any deep meaning in my life: school and church pagents, the circus, town parades. The actors need to be dressed in these somewhat outlandish, cartoonlike images so that the audience will know immediately that we are not about to witness a day in the life of this or that particular individual, but rather that we are being brought into the presence of archetypes (such as those that people our dreams) and, hence, ultimately into the presence of our selves.

The Set

In a space created communally by all the participants in the ritual are found objects: in the center, an old wooden table and four chairs — rough, hammered together; over the table, a hanging light bulb with a paper shade; in one corner, a bench with a working hot plate and a huge pot of soup; over this, on a wall, many pots, soup ladles, tin cups, bowls, spoons, etc.; in another corner, a chopping block with a double-headed ax (a sagaris) on it; over the block, a gigantic, blown-up photograph of Ann's Mom (actually a portrait of Ann about twenty-five years older). Above all this — hanging on wires from the ceiling or covering the walls — are dolls, every kind of doll imaginable: small, large, dressed, undressed, rag dolls, china dolls, headless dolls, old dolls, new dolls. On a higher level still, and visible to the audience, is Snake's domain, from which the lighting and the music can be directed by Snake and, again, in the sight of the audience. Snake's domain should be dominated by an altar on which stands an effigy of the Terrible Goddess of the Blood-Seed.

The Costumes: Suggested Images

The actors are dressed in secondhand, "found" clothes suggesting a circus or a school pageant. Ann wears an old bridal gown and flowers in her hair, while Myles dresses in a tattered tuxedo jacket, pants that are too big, suspenders, and sneakers. Carla wears large, false breasts, or a Mae West, along with full skirts, an apron, and boots; Vera a little girl's party dress — a very short skirt — and high heels. Dad's costume combines a tweed jacket and an old felt hat with sneakers and long johns. Snake wears a red, slinky gown, the headdress of a vulture, and bones; and her face is painted with a mask, extravagant and savage.

The Masks

The masks Vera and Carla use should be life-masks of the actors playing them, and these should be made up in exaggerated caricature of their roles — the coquette and the old crone. These two masks must be able to be burned during the performance of the play. Mom's mask, used by Snake, is the life-mask of the actor playing Ann made up to look twenty-five years older — like the photograph over the chopping block.

The Music

Except for the music accompanying Snake's primitive songs, the music should suggest folksongs, spirituals and blues, madrigals, lullabies and nursery rhymes. It should evoke a nostalgic sense of longing. The music may be played by the musicians alone, who may also join in the singing, or it my be played by the musicians and the actors, using all kinds of found or child-oriented instruments: drums and xylophones, saws and kazoos, recorders.

The Transitions

Transitions between the scenes can be marked with lighting, and/or music. The scene titles should be announced to the audience by Snake.

The Journal Readings

The readings are Ann's entry into another consciousness. They could be made from a particular part of the stage, set aside for Ann and her journal. They could be accompanied by sounds and slow movements made by other members of the cast and by the musicians, who can collectively create associative images for the readings. As the journal readings are related to the dream and other supraconscious worlds of all the participants, they are heightened moments in the ongoing ritual and should be treated as such.

— Martha Boesing

THE CHARACTERS

Ann
Myles, *her husband*
Carla, *her older sister*
Vera, *her younger sister*
Dad, *her father*
Snake, *the high priestess of the Terrible Goddess of the Blood-Seed*

THE PROLOGUE

The Wedding Procession

The play opens with a procession which is both holy and clownish. SNAKE *holds a huge, leather-bound book.*

ALL (*singing*):
    The winter was long,
    The river choked,
    The river choked.
    Men sat in the dark;
    Women were mute.
    No one spoke;
    No one breathed.
    Ann looked in the mirror,
    Ann hung her dolls on the wall.

SNAKE (*approaching* ANN; *she holds up* MOM'S *mask*):
    Psst! Annie! Annie! I got something for you . . . . It's a present.

ANN *takes the book from* SNAKE/MOM *without looking at her, as if she doesn't see her. She holds it close to herself all through the ceremony.*

ALL (*singing*):
    Ann goes to the wedding.
    The river is choked.
    No one breathes;
    No one speaks.
    The virgins go to the wedding.
    The old crones go to the wedding.
    The child who was lost
    Becomes the wife who is lost.

    Ann goes to the river.
    The river runs into her dreams.
    The river runs into her book;
    And there it begins.

ANN (*reading from the book*): From the journal: I walk to the river to watch the last of the snow melting away. I crouch down in the tall brown grass and stare out at the river. A creature rustles the grass behind me. I am startled. I turn to see him. He is a lizard, a long green lizard. He pays no attention to me. He makes his way through the grass to a clearing by the edge of the river. There he crawls into a small coffin which appears to be waiting there for him. I lean over and peer into the coffin. He looks merely asleep, not dead. On the surface of the water a face appears. It is the face of an old man with a forked tongue. He laughs at me. It is the face of God.

ANN *closes the book and looks up into the stony eyes of* SNAKE.

SNAKE: You write that?
ANN: Yes.
SNAKE: Ah-ha!
ANN: What do you mean by that? And who are you anyway? I didn't invite you to my wedding.
SNAKE: I'm your . . . mother!
ANN: Don't be absurd! My mother is dead, and you're not the least bit like her anyways.
SNAKE: All right! I'm not your mother if that's what you want to believe.
SNAKE *sings to* ANN *and to the audience.*

>I am the high priestess
>Of the Terrible Goddess
>Of the Blood-Seed!
>I am Snake.
>I am Sssssssnnnnnnnnak-k-k-ke!

>I know
>There is no happiness
>Without some sadness;
>There is no good intent
>Without some badness;
>I know there is no having
>Without some being had-ness;
>And there is no resurrection
>Without madness!

>I know!
>I know!
>In an age of mass oppression
>And severely felt repression,
>There is limited indiscretion,
>And the merest dark suggestion
>Can give you indiges-tion!
>I know!
>I know!
>In a time of mass denial
>There is little respect for guile,
>The darkness is reviled

And evil is defiled!
I know!
I know!
But I'm telling you this without a smile:
It spoils my style!

I hold the wisdom of the universe in my hand;
I am the guardian of all pestilence in the land;
I despise the productivity of the bland;
And on the empty skulls of Sodom
I take my stand.
I am the high priestess
Of the Terrible Goddess
Of the Blood-Seed

I am the thorn in your flesh,
The snake in the grass,
The skeleton in your closet,
And the itch up your ass!
I am malevolence, depravity, and vice!
I am everything
That isn't very nice!

Virulent witches,
Angry sisters,
Take your pick:
Join me
And be a brute,
Or — stay sick!

ANN *stares at her, startled and mystified.*

Scene 1

In Which Ann Is Given to Myles in Wedlock

SNAKE *plays the part of the Preacher.* VERA *and* CARLA *are* ANN'S *attendants. The wedding begins.*

DAD (*clears his throat, nervously*): I am here to present my offspring, my little daughter. When she was a child our relationship was warmed by a particular and rather unusual mood of closeness and conviviality. I often bounced her upon my knee.

CARLA (*aside to* VERA): It's true.

VERA (*aside to* CARLA): It's not! It was me he bounced on his knee!

DAD: I taught her to be independent, resilient, reliable, and self-assured . . .

CARLA (*aside to* VERA): Ha! I was the one had to learn those lessons! She never learned one of them. Not one!

DAD: . . . all while maintaining a sense of security and protectiveness issuing from me to her; in short, I held her hand when she crossed the street.

CARLA (*aside to* VERA): And now I have to hold her hand when she crosses the room!

DAD: I encouraged her talents and artistic sensitivities, promoting opportunities for her to remove the bushel basket, so to speak, and let her light shine abroad in the world. Frequently, from time to time, I sat in the school auditorium and listened to her sing.

VERA (*aside to* CARLA): It was me that sang! She was too scared! She got me to do it. What's the matter with him? His memory going?

CARLA: Sssssssshhhh!

DAD: I have essayed my best to be a dedicated teacher, an impartial guide, an understanding father. It is with not a little ambivalence — a sense of confusion *and* a deep pride, a touch of reluctance *and* much eagerness — that I present, therefore, my little daughter, my Ann. Here she is, Myles; I give her to you. (*Pause.*) I pray that this is not a farewell to my daughter, but a greeting to my son. (*They shake hands.*)

ANN (*suddenly starts: She thinks she has heard* MOM *call her*): Mom?

MYLES: What is it, Ann?

ANN: I thought I heard Mom calling.

MYLES: You're imagining things again, Ann. Your Mom's dead.

ANN: I know. (*Softly.*) I know.

MYLES: You okay, Honey?

ANN: Yeh . . . yeh . . . sure . . . I'm okay.

MYLES: You're okay.

ANN: That's what I just said.

MYLES: It's all gonna be okay.

SNAKE: May we proceed?

MYLES: Proceed? Yes . . . of course . . . proceed.

SNAKE (*chanting*):
    In the beginning is the end.
    In the beginning is the end.
    In the beginning is the end.
    Do you Myles take this woman?

MYLES: I do.
SNAKE: Ann?
ANN: Yes?
SNAKE (*Pause*): I do?
ANN: I do.
SNAKE: The world is falling apart at the seams!
DAD: Falling apart at the seams? Not a totally undeniable statement. There is a certain foundering, an absence of direction, a kind of dancing atop the treadmill which threatens collapse, to be sure. But there are those faithful rocks we can still depend upon. Thank God. (*He crosses to* CARLA, *pats her on the back.*)
SNAKE: The streets are running with blood!
DAD: Running with blood? Too desperate a metaphor, perhaps, reminiscent of the sordid themes executed in our theaters these days.
SNAKE: The men are raping the women!
DAD: Raping the women . . . ? Hmmmm . . . . Certainly succumbing to temptations of a violent and turbulent society which has unfortunately neglected to educate its sons in the art of love. (*He affectionately chucks* VERA *under the chin.*)
SNAKE: The women are castrating the men, ha, ha!
DAD: Castrating the men . . . ! A disproportionate and rather extreme insinuation, albeit . . . .
SNAKE (*interrupting*): It's a good time to get married!
DAD: True enough! It is that. It's a good time to get married.
VERA (*shaking* ANN's *hand*): A good time to get married.
SNAKE (*puts on* MOM's *mask*): A good time to get married, Honey!
MYLES (*caressing her reassuringly*): A good time to get married.
SNAKE: This day, Ann, you are possessed. You belong to the world of the dam . . . uh . . . saved! Congratulations!
ALL (*singing, except* ANN *who dances awkwardly like a child on display*):

> She is saved!
>   Doesn't she look pretty!
> She's possessed!
>   Dressed all in white!
> She belongs!
>   Such a lovely bride!
> She is married!
>   Such a pretty sight!
> Alleluja! Alleluja!

SNAKE: You may kiss her, Myles. Kiss-kiss-kiss. (*They kiss.* VERA *giggles.* CARLA *smiles benignly.*)

Scene 2

In Which Myles Is Introduced to Vera and Carla and the Intrigue Begins

MYLES *grabs* ANN *up in his arms and swings her around. He carries her into the space.*

MYLES: Well . . . here we are!

ANN: Yes. It isn't much, but it's . . . .

MYLES: Home. (*They both laugh.* MYLES *looks around.*) It's real different, Ann — all the dolls and things all over the walls. Real different . . . . I mean, it's pretty . . . . kinda . . . . pretty.

ANN: You don't have to like it, Myles. We don't have to live here always.

MYLES: It's fine, Ann. Fine. (*He kisses her. Suddenly he notices* VERA *and* CARLA *standing behind the table.*) Hey, hey, hey — what have we here? Who're they?

ANN: They're my sisters, Myles. You know that.

VERA *curtsies to* MYLES. CARLA *shakes hands.*

MYLES: I do?

ANN: You remember Vera, Myles. When I couldn't go to the dance and I said it was because I had to stay home with my kid sister and you said bring her along? Remember? You wanted to dance all night with her. Don't you remember, Myles?

MYLES: Oh . . .yes . . .yes . . .right. You're a damn' good dancer, Vera. Now I remember. We had a good time that night, didn't we?

MYLES *laughs.* VERA *giggles appreciatively.*

ANN: And Carla, Myles. Remember Carla? She came over and took care of you that night . . . in the winter? When you were sick. She went out in that terrible storm even though she didn't want to. How could you forget that, Myles? She made the fire. Remember?

MYLES: Oh, yeh . . . yes. I guess I do. Wellll . . . . (*Laughs.*) Hello. Come by for a visit?

ANN: Well, actually, Myles, they . . .

MYLES: Actually, I think you'd both understand, being Ann's sisters and all . . . . You'd understand, wouldn't you, if we just . . . ? Well, I don't mean to be rude, but we'd like to be alone, just gettin' married and all.

ANN: They live here, Myles.

MYLES: They live here? In your home?

ANN: Yes .... It's their home, too.

MYLES: Why didn't you tell me this, Ann?

ANN: Well, I was afraid to. I was afraid you'd say no. And I knew you didn't have the money to get our own place and I was afraid you might call it all off or something, and ... oh, Myles, I just kind of hoped it'd all be okay.

MYLES: Well, it's not okay. (*Pause.*) What do you mean by okay?

ANN: Carla does all the cooking, Myles, and she cleans the house and Vera ... well, Vera ... dances! Remember? They won't get in the way, Myles. You'll see. You'll grow to love them even more than I do, I'm sure, Myles. Really. Please, Myles, don't spoil it. Don't spoil everything.

SNAKE, DAD, MUSICIANS (*any or all of them sing*):

> Terrible is the yearning to be loving;
> Terrible, too, is the longing to be good.
> Marriage is a most disasterous journey,
> For any who wish to avoid being misunderstood.

MYLES: Okay, Ann, okay. We'll try it.

CARLA (*sets out four mugs and pours wine from a jug*): Come on, you two! It's the first night; the night of "nuptial bliss!" Not a night for squabbling. Enjoy yourselves! (*She raises her cup.*) To marriage!

MYLES: It'll be okay, Ann. (*He takes a cup.*) To marriage! (*He puts his arm around* ANN.) Carla .... (*He drinks to her.*) Vera .... (*He drinks to her.*)

CARLA: Well, I just want to say I think it's wonderful. I always knew Annie'd find herself a nice guy some day and that it'd all turn out just fine. And I want to say I think she got the best. Welcome, Myles. Welcome home!

MYLES *looks down at his feet, embarrassed, but obviously liking the attention. They all drink to* MYLES.

CARLA: Say something, Vera!

VERA (*giggling, coyly*): Oh, I don't know what to say. (*Pause.*) He's real cute, Annie. (*She raises her cup and drinks, eyeing* MYLES.)

CARLA (*poking* VERA): Give her the gifts, Vera.

VERA: Oh! Do I have to?

CARLA: Vera!

VERA (*talks with a sing-song, babyish voice*): Oooooooh! I suppose I have to! (*She giggles. She brings out two bundles wrapped in newspaper.*) Here, Ann — from me and Carla. I hope you like them very much.

ANN *opens the gifts and finds* VERA'S *and* CARLA'S *masks. She lifts them out and looks at them carefully. She is stunned. There is a terrible and very long silence. Finally* MYLES *breaks it.*

MYLES: What is it, Ann? Let's see.
ANN: It's only a joke.
VERA: It's not a joke, Ann!
CARLA: They'll bring you luck.
ANN: I don't want them!
CARLA: Someday you'll need them.
VERA: You might find them useful, Annie. (*She peeks coyly out through her mask at* MYLES. *He laughs.*) See?
ANN: I don't want them, Vera!
VERA: Okay, Annie, okay. Don't get all edgy about it!
ANN: And don't call me Annie. I'm not a baby any more!
VERA: Sorry . . . Ann!

>VERA *puts up her mask and performs a bizarre little dance and curtsies.* MYLES *laughs again.*

CARLA (*she has been setting out bowls, filling them with soup from the huge crock on the hot plate*): There, there, there. Stop all the fussing. You're embarrassing Myles. Sit down, both of you. We don't want to give away all the family secrets on Myles' first night here, do we? (*She jovially nudges* MYLES.) Have some soup. You must be famished, Myles. Eat. Eat!
SNAKE/MOM (*reading from* ANN's *journal with* MOM's *mask on*): From the journal: I wake up early before the sun. It will soon be ended I think, this long night. I light the candle and slip out of bed. Goose bumps pop out all over my skin. Today I will turn into a wife, I think, like the toad who turned into a prince! I take my wedding dress off its hanger and lift it over my head. It slips heavily over my body and, as it reaches my thighs, it transforms into hardening cement. I become fixed in stone, sealed in. Where the satin train had once been, there is now a huge white cat, sculpted in ivory, curled around my feet, his enormous eyes watching me. I know that he will devour me if either one of us moves. (*Looking up from the book.*) This musta been written in the dark. I can't make heads or tails of it!
ANN (*taking the book from* SNAKE/MOM *and reading*): I walk into the church. The pews are filled with ancient women. They are keening. They are mourning the loss of their daughters. At the altar stands the most beautiful man I have ever seen. He is an angel. His wings spread out across the church nave. He is enormous. I go to him. He puts his arms around me and holds my head against his chest. The wide, white feathers of his wings brush against my face. He is impervious to the moaning of the women.

Scene 3

In Which Carla Listens to Myles and Vera Discovers the Difficulty of Living with a Man

They are sitting at the table, eating soup, bread. They eat in silence for awhile.

CARLA: Tell us about yourself, Myles.
MYLES: Nothing much to tell.
CARLA: Oh, I'm sure that's not true. I'm sure you have many fascinating tales to tell, adventures, success stories.

They both laugh goodnaturedly.

MYLES: Once I won the state championship in basketball.
CARLA: See? What'd I tell you. A born hero.
MYLES (*laughs*): And I got the Boy Scout medal of honor. I saved this blind woman's life once. She was crossing right out in front of a car. Didn't see it coming. I whisked right out there and pulled her away from the car. Almost got run over myself. (*Laughs. Shakes his head.*) I was only twelve. I was a hero then. For a while.
CARLA: I knew it.
MYLES: Knew what?
CARLA: I could tell it in your eyes. You're a good man, Myles, a good, loving man. (MYLES *laughs shyly.*) You got yourself a good man, Annie. Just like Dad.
ANN: Dad??!!
CARLA: Oh, now, he talks a lot, blabbers on and on, but he loves you, Annie. He'd do anything for you in the world. He's a kind man. A kind and generous man.
ANN: Well, Myles and Dad are not the *least* bit alike, no matter how you look at it, Carla, and I think that's a ridiculous comparison to make, anyway.
VERA: Dad ain't anywhere near as sexy!
CARLA: Vera!
MYLES (*laughs*): It's okay, Ann. I think Carla was paying me a compliment.
CARLA: Of course I was. (*Pause.*) Eat.

There is a silence.

ANN (*out of the silence*): It seems kinda sad to me. Nobody seems to really know anything about anything.
MYLES: What?
ANN: What?

MYLES: What were you saying?

ANN: Saying? Was I saying something?

CARLA: Don't pay no mind to her, Myles. She daydreams. You know, kinda goes off into a reverie or something. She's done it ever since she was a little girl. You mustn't worry your head about it. I'll keep an eye out for her.

Silence. They finish eating.

VERA (*rising*): Well, if you'll all please excuse me, I'm going to get ready for bed now. (*She goes to the corner and starts undressing. She sings.*) "Sleepy-time Gal, I've got those sleepy-time blues.... Sleepy-time Gal...."

Pause while she dresses and no one speaks.

Rooty-toot-toot
Said the millionaire;
Don't look now,
'Cause I'm all bare!

She giggles.

CARLA: Vera!

MYLES: Ann, shouldn't your sister . . . I mean, isn't there any place for her to get undressed besides here?

CARLA: Vera, turn around. You're embarrassing Myles.

MYLES: Ann?

ANN (*snapping out of her reverie*): Yes?

MYLES: Vera is . . . .

ANN: Oh, don't bother about Vera, Myles. She always dresses in the kitchen. It's warmer.

MYLES: It's different now.

ANN: Different?

MYLES: I'm here, Honey. It isn't the same.

CARLA: Vera, you're bothering Myles.

VERA: I am? Oh, don't bother 'bout me, Myles. I'm just doin' what I always do, you know, doin' what comes natchurly. I mean, don't you pay any attention to little old me. You go on doin' whatever it is you're doin', and I'll just go on living like you weren't here. I mean, it's *won*-derful that you are here, but . . . oh, you know what I mean!

CARLA: Just finish up and get on into bed, Vera.

VERA (*turning around in a frilly and revealing nightgown*): Like my new gown, Ann? I got it specially because of you . . . and Myles. Because it was your wedding night. (*She curtsies awkwardly and giggles.*) Well . . . guess I'll just say g'night, Carla. G'night. G'night, Ann. Good night, Myles. (*To* ANN.) Doesn't he look sorta like Paul Newman?

VERA *offers her cheek for a kiss to* MYLES. MYLES *hesitates, then kisses it awkwardly. She leaves.*

CARLA: Guess I'll check out. You two be sure to lock up and shut out the lights. Behave yourselves. (*She winks and laughs good-naturedly.*)
MYLES: Goodnight, Carla. Thanks for the food . . . and the talk.
ANN: G'night.
CARLA: It was nothin', Myles, nothin'. (*She leaves. From off:*) Pleasant dreams. Sleep well!

Pause.

MYLES: I don't think it'll work, Ann.
ANN: What won't work?
MYLES: Us living here with them.
ANN: Oh, let's not get started on that again, Myles. (*Pause.*) You were having a good time. You were laughing! Besides, we can move if it gets too much.
MYLES: Okay, okay. I was laughing. That's true. Carla is very sweet and kind. And (*chuckles seductively*) Vera's not a bad sort. (*Pause.*) And we're here. That's what matters.

He pulls her down in his lap. They kiss.

MYLES: How will we know when it gets "too much"?
ANN (*thinks for a moment*): You'll look at me and say, "What's for dinner, Carla?" or "Give us a kiss, Vera!" Then it'll be too much.

They both laugh and embrace.

DAD, SNAKE, VERA, CARLA, MUSICIANS (*any or all of them sing*):

> Marvelous is the masquerade of lovers;
> Marvelous, too, the game of blind man's bluff.
> When love is the food of life, and you are starving,
> A million times twenty embraces is never enough.

Scene 4

In Which Myles Loses His Keys and Carla Finds Them

MYLES *enters and begins looking for something. He looks on the table, on the stove, behind the chairs, in his pants pockets. Finally he starts looking inside and behind the dolls and other things hanging on the walls. He appears dazed.* ANN *watches.*

ANN (*finally*): What's the matter, Myles?
MYLES (*without looking at her*): I've lost them! I can't find them! They're gone! They're lost! I'm lost! I'm nowhere without them!
ANN: Without what?
MYLES: The keys! The keys, the keys, the keys!
ANN: When did you last have them?
MYLES: Yesterday.
ANN: Where? In your hand? In your pocket?
MYLES: Look, Ann, they're gone! I've tried all that recall stuff. Either help me hunt for them or go away. They're lost. L-o-s-t-lost Don't just stand there asking stupid questions. The keys are gone.

ANN *joins* MYLES' *hunt for the keys. They build up the momentum into a pitch of desperation, tearing dolls and other objects off the wall, throwing discarded items into a pile in the center of the floor which begins to expand into a mound of junk, looking like a rat's nest. After a time,* CARLA *enters. She looks over the scene wordlessly. She crosses to* MYLES, *reaches into his left shirt pocket, removes the keys and hands them to him.* MYLES *stares at her for a moment, then takes the keys, chagrined.* CARLA *tousles his hair affectionately and laughs goodnaturedly.* MYLES *laughs back, relaxing. He leaves.* ANN *looks at* CARLA. *They begin to clean up the mess, placing things back on the wall.* ANN *gives up, sighs, sits at the table looking out vacantly.* CARLA *continues cleaning. She enjoys it.*

SNAKE (*reading*): From the journal: I am sitting at the kitchen table. Myles suddenly looks up and announces that the world is coming to an end. At that very moment two black crows fly in through the kitchen window and start pecking and grabbing at the bread lying on the table. Caw! Caw! Caw! they screech. I scream at them to stop, but they pay no attention to me. Caw! Caw! Caw! It seems to go on for a long time, but I think it is only a moment before Myles is standing over me. I think he has struck my face. The crows have stopped their cawing. I get up and walk over to the window. In the back yard by the river path, a gigantic yellow crocus has sprung up. It must be at least three feet tall. Its petals are still folded up — like hands praying.

SCENE 5

In Which Ann Sings a Song for Her Mom

CARLA *is sweeping and cleaning.* ANN *and* VERA *sit at the table.* ANN *is writing in her journal.* VERA *is polishing her nails.*

CARLA: Feet. (*She sweeps under* ANN'S *feet.*)
VERA: Watcha writin', Annie? Let's see!
ANN: None of your business.
CARLA (*to* VERA): Feet. (*She sweeps under* VERA'S *feet.*)
VERA: Hear that, Carla? She's writin' 'bout us, betcha.
CARLA: I'm sure she's got better things to write about, Vera. Leave her alone.
VERA: Myles is nice, Annie, real nice. (*No response.* ANN *goes on writing.*)
CARLA (*to* ANN): Arms. (*She sponges the table under* ANN'S *arms.*)
VERA: I said: Myles is nice.
CARLA: She don't care what you think about Myles, Vera. Arms. (*She sponges the table under* VERA'S *arms.*)
VERA: Sure would like to know what yer writin' there.
CARLA: Why don't you take care of your own business, Vera, like she said. Find something nice to do. Make some pretty thing like you do. To go in the center of the table. For Myles. (VERA *doesn't respond.*) But whatever you do, you mind your own business and let Annie mind hers.
ANN (*with a sudden burst of emotion*): She hasn't minded her own business since the day she was born!
VERA (*laughs*): Remember that little box you had? You sure were mad when I figured out how to open it! (*No response.* ANN *returns to her writing. She glares at* VERA. *Suddenly* VERA *pulls the book away from* ANN *and begins to read aloud from it.*) "It is raining. I am walking through a long tunnel. I don't know where I am heading. It is dark. I think I am lost . . ." Brother!

That's the understatement of the year!
ANN (*lunges for the book*): Give it back!
CARLA (*takes the book from* VERA *and gives it back to* ANN): Stop the fighting, you two. Be nice. What's the matter with you?
VERA: You hate me, don'tcha Annie?
ANN: Don't call me Annie!
VERA: Think I care? Do you think I care?
CARLA: I said to stop it!
ANN (*pause*): Carla, don't you ever want anything from anybody? I mean, don't you ever just feel like crying? Or just sitting still?
CARLA: Now who'd get all the work done if I gave in to that kind of snivelling?
VERA: She's always been like that — long's I can remember.
CARLA: And where would you be today, Miss Hoighty-toit, if I sat around all day polishin' my nails and standin' in front of the mirror?
ANN: Now you're fighting! I don't understand either of you! I don't understand you one bit!
VERA (*pause*): Myles likes us anyways.
ANN: Myles? . . . Yes, I suppose he does.
CARLA (*turning on* ANN): Lucky for him we're here, I'd say. Place would fall apart without us. A man needs a woman. Needs someone to take care of him proper. (*Pause, and then somewhat begrudgingly.*) Someone to play with him, too, I suppose.
ANN (*cries*): Oh!
VERA (*tauntingly*): Cry-baby! Cry-baby!
CARLA: Oh, I'm sorry, Annie. I'm sorry. I lost my head. I didn't know what I was saying. (*Holds her and rocks her.*)
ANN: Leave me alone, Carla. Oh, both of you, leave me alone!
CARLA: Okay, Annie. It's okay. We'll leave you alone. (*She signals* VERA *to leave.*) I'll be here, Annie. I'll be here if you need me. (*To* VERA.) She don't know what's good for her. She don't know whether she's comin' or goin'. (VERA *and* CARLA *exit.*)
ANN (*singing*):

> O, Mama, I'm a goin' 'cross that lonesome vale;
> Wind's a-sighin'
> Whole world's set a-cryin'
> In that first baby's wail.
>
> O, Mama, O, Mama, can'tcha hear my cry?
> Birds a-wingin'
> I need to hear you singin'
> One last lullaby.

Scene 6

In Which Vera Seduces Myles

MYLES *enters the kitchen. Only* VERA *is there.*

MYLES: Hi, Vera.
VERA: Well . . . hello!
MYLES: Where's Carla and Ann?
VERA: Dunno. (*Pause.*) Won't I do?
MYLES: Sure, Vera. Sure, you'll do. (*He sits down. Pause.*) Watcha been doin'?
VERA: Sittin'.
MYLES: Hmmmmm. (*Pause.*) Whew! I'm dog tired.
VERA: I can imagine. Workin' all day. (*Pause.* VERA *laughs out loud.*)
MYLES: What's so funny?
VERA: I was just rememberin' once when I was a kid, I climbed up in a big old maple tree we had in the back yard and a couple o' boys who lived 'round our house were standin' at the bottom of the tree lookin' up. Only I didn't have any underpants on, see? And they started laughin' and pointin' up at me, so instead of gettin' all flustered 'bout it, which I could have done real easy, I just leaned over the limb of the old maple tree and I called down to all of them:

> The Queen of Sheba went to a dance,
> But she forgot to wear her pants.
> All the king's horses and all the king's men
> Couldn't get Sheba to put her pants on again!

MYLES (*laughing*): What did they do then?
VERA: Who?
MYLES: The boys standin' under the tree.
VERA: Well . . . what would you have done, Myles?
MYLES (*laughs, gets up, looks around*): Wonder what's keepin' those two so long?
VERA: Don't you think it's time we stopped playing games, Myles?
MYLES: Games?
VERA: Well, it seems obvious to me that we are very attracted to one another, you to me . . . and . . . me to you. I was thinkin' maybe we should just simply get on with it.
MYLES: I guess I don't know what you're talkin' about, Vera.
VERA: No? Well, let's put it this way: Ann is my sister and I know for a certain

fact that she won't be givin' you what you need — what any man needs — and I thought as a kind of sisterly favor . . . I mean, it only seems fair, me and Carla living here and all, that we ought to do our very best to help out. (*Pause.* MYLES *stares at her.*) Now, don't you worry 'bout Ann, Myles, don't you worry. I'm sure she won't mind. She won't mind at all . . . .

VERA *undresses* MYLES *very slowly and* MYLES *succumbs to* VERA'S *powers of seduction while the others sing.*

DAD, SNAKE, CARLA, MUSICIANS (*any or all of them sing*):

> Innocent is the wish to be devoted;
> Innocent, too, the wish to be a friend.
> Men harbor the hope of returning again to the womb;
> Both treason and lust spring out of this hope in the end.

ANN (*reading*): From the journal: Myles stares at me across the table through black water. I reach out for him but the water is too thick. I leap into the water but sink down under its surface. I think I am drowning. Each time I come up for some air, the waves push against my face forcing me under again. In the distance I see Myles beckoning to me. He is smiling as if he has not noticed that we are creatures who drown when we're cut off from air.

SCENE 7

In Which Myles Predicts the End of the World
and Ann Relives Her Dream

MYLES, ANN, VERA, CARLA *are all sitting around the kitchen table.* CARLA *is serving.*

CARLA (*to* MYLES): Eat. (*He accepts her handout. To* ANN.) Eat. (ANN *covers her bowl with her hand.*) What's the matter with you, Annie, you gotta eat.

MYLES: Leave her alone.

CARLA: Leave her alone? She's gonna starve herself. She's been sittin' at the table like this for days.

MYLES: I know, Carla. I'm worried about her.

CARLA: Well, now, I didn't mean to worry you. She'll be fine. It's just the excitement of getting married and all that. Long as some of us can still move around we'll be fine.

VERA: Fuss, fuss, fuss!

MYLES: The world's coming to an end.

CARLA: What?

MYLES: The world's coming to an end. I read about it in this morning's paper.

CARLA: What on earth are you talking about, Myles?

MYLES: Old man. Lives in the mountains. Said he had a vision. The world's coming to an end.

CARLA: I don't think it's a good idea to believe that kind of stuff.

MYLES: Why not? He ran all the way down the mountain side to tell the people who lived below.

CARLA: And a lot of good that did! What can they do about it? Even if it is true. We still have to go on living, have to go on making ends meet. (*Casting a pointed look at* VERA.) At least some of us do.

VERA: Oh, Carla, what a grouch! You'd love it if the world came to an end. You'd be sitting upstairs with the angels singing, "Halleluja! I told you so!" I s'pose.

CARLA (*pointedly, to* VERA): Maybe the world would be a better place if we all were dead.

VERA: What a crab!

CARLA: Hussy!

VERA: Crab!

ANN (*softly*): Stop it! (*Loudly.*) Stop it! (*She puts her hands over her ears.*)

SNAKE *enters to change the scene into the dream.*

ANN (*reading*): From the journal: I am dreaming. Snake is in my dream. And Vera and Carla. They are all here. Snake is moving the kitchen furniture around, placing the chairs in a row.

SNAKE *sets three of the chairs to the left of the kitchen table.*

She is putting an ugly old satin sheet over the table. It once was white; now it's torn.

SNAKE *clears the table and covers it with a satin sheet.*

Snake is taking the shade from the kitchen lamp.

She does so.

The light bulb is bare and makes our warm kitchen look like an operating room in a hospital.

SNAKE *seats* VERA *and* CARLA *in two of the chairs.*

Vera and Carla sit down in the chairs. I am watching them, but they don't seem to see me at all. Myles is there, too.

SNAKE *puts a white hospital gown on* MYLES *and ties it in the back. She gives him a surgical face mask and a pair of surgical gloves which he puts on.*

He has on a white gown and a mask over his face. And Dad is here. He looks right through me as if I were only a vapor.

ANN *closes the book.* SNAKE *seats* DAD *in the third chair. She gives him a drum. He begins to beat it with a slow, steady pulsing. He continues to beat it throughout the dream, increasing the tempo almost imperceptibly until the end.*

Everything is done with utmost economy. People move as if they are traveling through water.

SNAKE *places a naked doll on the table which she gets from the wall.* SNAKE *and* MYLES *dissect the doll, removing the limbs, head, hair as one might break open a shellfish before eating it.* MYLES *works with dispassion,* SNAKE *with obvious enthusiasm. When they have finished their task,* CARLA *falls from her chair onto the floor with a swift and economical movement. She remains in a heap for the rest of the dream.*

SNAKE *places the broken pieces of the doll in an old brown paper sack. She presents this to* ANN *who clutches it to her for the rest of the dream.*

SNAKE *brings* ANN *to the table. She places her there as a nurse would place a pregnant woman on an operating table, pushing her feet up against her hips, knees up, legs open. She covers her pelvis with a piece of dirty white sheeting.*

SNAKE *gives* MYLES *an oversized pair of scissors. He cuts the sheet lying over* ANN *as if he were cutting open the skin of her abdomen. When he is finished,* VERA *falls off her chair onto the floor.*

MYLES *slowly removes a bright red satin ribbon — the kind used on Christmas wreaths — from between* ANN'S *legs. It is yards long.* SNAKE *gathers it. When he is finished, he removes the rubber gloves.*

MYLES *and* SNAKE *set* ANN *up and wrap her pelvis in the ribbon, over her dress, between her legs, around her hips, like a diaper. They bind it off tightly, tying it in back.*

MYLES *and* SNAKE *sit* ANN *up on the edge of the table.* SNAKE *brings a wooden bowl with* CARLA'S *soup.* MYLES *raises it to* ANN'S *mouth. She drinks.* MYLES *washes his hands in the bowl of soup and dries them on a towel offered by* SNAKE.

The light has dimmed. The only light left is the bare light bulb over the table. SNAKE *sets it in motion.*

MYLES *removes his gown. He leaves.* SNAKE *leaves. The light swings back and forth.* ANN *sits on the edge of the table clutching the brown paper sack in her hands. The drum continues.*

ANN *opens her mouth to scream. No sound comes out. The drum beat stops abruptly.*

The light swings back and forth.

The light dims out. Blackness.

As the lights come up, ANN *is struggling to unbind the ribbon.*

MYLES: Ann! Ann! What's the matter? How did you get like this?
VERA: Don't look at me!
MYLES: Give me a hand, Carla. How'd she get like this? (*They begin to untie the ribbon.*)
CARLA: Must have been one of her nightmares.
MYLES: Nightmares?
CARLA: Yeh. She's had them ever since she was a kid. Sometimes she gets up and walks around the house, sometimes she does strange things to herself — dresses up, smears dirt on herself, sometimes she ties herself up. Like this.
MYLES: Don't you think we should get her some kind of help?
CARLA: She's always okay afterwards. Nice as she ever was. They don't seem to really bother her too much. The nightmares, I mean.

They finish untying the ribbon. ANN *is still clutching the sack.*

MYLES: Ann?
VERA: She sure looked crazy tied up in that ribbon!
CARLA: Vera! Be nice now!

ANN *seems catatonic.* MYLES *slaps her face.*

MYLES: Ann!

ANN (*comes to, looks around at everyone*): I'm okay. I was dreaming. I'm sorry. I'm terribly sorry!
MYLES: Nothin' to be sorry about, Honey. You're okay.
ANN: That's what I just said. I'm okay.
MYLES: Everything's okay.

CARLA brings two mugs of wine. She brushes ANN's hair back. She rubs MYLES' back. MYLES sits. They drink. Silence. After a time, MYLES gets up.

MYLES: Well . . . .
CARLA: Leaving?
MYLES: Leaving. Gotta go to work.
VERA: Give me a kiss goodbye.

He does, perfunctorily. VERA pouts.

MYLES: Bye, Ann. (*He starts to kiss her, stops himself.*) You'll be okay.
VERA: I think she's crazy.
MYLES *and* CARLA: She's okay!!

CARLA takes VERA off.

Very slowly ANN gets up and looks out at the audience. She sees them as if for the first time. They seem very beautiful to her, like the crocus in her journal. She tosses the paper sack out into the audience.

Scene 8

In Which Myles Asks Ann to Change Her Ways

MYLES *and* ANN *sit at the table.*

MYLES: Ann, somethin's gotta give. Somethin's gotta change. I'm worried about you, Honey. You should try to get into something, do something, move around, be somebody.

(*Pause.*)

You should be like Carla. You know, clean the house or sweep the floor or cook the soup or wash the dishes or water the plants. You should try that, Ann. It would make you feel better. Carla likes doing all that. You might like it, too, Ann.

Pause.

Or you should be like Vera. Do your nails or curl your hair or dress up pretty. Be silly sometimes. Have a little fun. You should try that, Ann. You'd feel better.

Pause.

A man needs a woman who can do those things. A man needs a woman like that, Ann.

Pause.

Ann? . . . . You're my girl . . . Right?
ANN: I'll try, Myles. I'll try.

Pause.

MYLES: Maybe it's time to go, Honey. Move into a new house.

Pause.

Or they could go, Ann. I could find them a new house. Is that what you'd like?
ANN: No, Myles. I'll be okay. They can stay. They can stay.
SNAKE (*reading*): From the journal: I am in a cave. Vera is leaning against the wall. Her hair is matted. She has on a grey, tattered dress. She has no shoes. She is tearing the flesh on her legs with her long nails. It is falling off in chunks. Carla is sweeping the floor of the cave. She, too, is dressed in grey rags, her hair matted and her feet bare like Vera's. She is laughing. She is sweeping everything out of the cave. She thinks I am a heap of old papers. She sweeps me into the pile of garbage she has collected. I know that I am in Hell.
MYLES: Maybe the book's no good for you, Ann. Maybe you should let it go for a while, forget about it for a few days.

Pause.

What do you think, Ann?

Pause.

Why don't you say something? . . . Anything.

MYLES *shakes her. He sighs. He lays his head on his arms.*

Scene 9

In Which Ann Reads Aloud from Her Journal to Dad

DAD *and* MYLES *are in the kitchen.* ANN *enters.*

ANN: Hello, Dad.

DAD: It's been quite a while, Ann, a time ruled by the details of daily routines if you know what I mean. I have often thought of you and felt a great concern for you rising up within my breast, bringing with it an almost uncontrollable urge to contact you, to assure myself of your well-being.

ANN: Why didn't you call, Dad?

DAD: Ah, well . . . you know . . . time! Time! You understand how these impulses occur and slip out of our hands almost before we have had occasion to understand their meaning.

ANN: Yeh. Sure, Dad.

DAD: But now I am here! Now I am standing here in my little daughter's home. Tell me all about what's been happening: your activities, your progress with your marriage, your plans for the future!

ANN: I don't know about any of those things, Dad. I want to tell you about what I've been feeling lately.

DAD: Your emotional life is truly important to me, Ann. I want you to understand that. But feelings are never experienced in a void, you know. I need to know the facts of the case, the extenuating circumstances so to speak, before I can fully grasp the more elusive sensibilities lying beneath them.

ANN: Dad, listen to me! I don't know why I'm feeling like I do. The "extenuating circumstances" don't make any sense to me! I'm sad. All the time sad. There isn't any reason for it that I can figure out. I cry a lot, Dad, like when Mom died. Can you hear what I'm saying? I want you to help me, Dad!

DAD: Well . . . it's not exactly in my hands, anymore, dear. I'm sure that Myles and Vera and Carla are all deeply concerned about this temporary melancholy of yours, as I am, too. I am, too. We all want to listen to you, as you say, and offer as much support as we can within the framework of our own occupations and responsibilities. Remember, Sweetie, this, too, like all things, will pass. We all have to ride the crests and troughs of life's tremulous albeit exacting waves, trying to avoid the pits of despair along the way. "It is not for us to question why, merely to do . . . or die!" . . . Is that right? I'm not certain that I got it exactly right.

ANN: Dad, Myles, listen. Will you let me read something to you? Something I wrote?

MYLES: Sure, Ann, I'd like to hear it. I'd really like to hear it.
DAD: Any composition of yours is always a delight to my ears, Sweetie.
MYLES: Go on, Honey, read it.

SNAKE *brings the journal to* ANN.

SNAKE: Lots o' luck, Honey.
ANN: I'm going to open this book up and read the first thing I come to, regardless of what it says. Do you understand? I write here every day. Sometimes I write awful things. But I'm going to read whatever I come to, no matter what it is! (*She reads.*) I am walking up the stairs of my house. There is a terrible stillness everywhere. Nothing stirs, not even the air. I feel frightened, as if something catastrophic is about to happen. I walk into Vera's and Carla's bedroom. They are lying on their beds — dead. They have been murdered. Someone has come into their room. Their hands and their feet have been chopped off with an ax. Their bellies have been torn open. There is blood everywhere, gushing out of them. It has stained the sheets and the comforter. The color of the red blood swims in front of my eyes. I am suddenly swept into a red wind. It is a tornado. It carries me into the air with a violent gust. I am carried on the red wind out of their room, down the stairs and through the house. I am tossed onto the floor of the kitchen. The silence engulfs me. I know I must never tell anyone what I have seen.

ANN *looks up at* MYLES *and* DAD. *There is a long and terrible silence.*

DAD (*finally breaking the silence*): Well . . . an imaginative and fanciful piece of writing, Ann. I'm sure that it contains certain exaggerations dwelt upon for the sake of the imagery.

Pause.

It occurs to me that you should perhaps get out a little more, go visiting, engage in conversations with people — normal people — who exist outside the boundaries of your rather protected and sheltered world. Don't you think?

Long pause.

Have you perhaps been reading too many Gothic novels, Ann?

Pause.

Well . . . well . . . forgive me, but I must curtail this visit. I have treatises, contracts, documents, . . . er . . . you know: All in a day's work! Goodbye, Myles, wonderful seeing you again. We mustn't let it be so long next time. Forgive me, Ann. (*He looks at her for a long moment.*) Forgive me . . . forgive me. (*He leaves.*)

ANN *and* MYLES *look at each other. She crosses to him and puts her arms around him, seeking comfort.* MYLES *pauses for a slight moment and then embraces her. She cries in his arms while* DAD *sings his song.*

DAD (*sings*):

    A man has only one fugitive season
    To teach all that he's learned to his daughter.
    He gives her his best pearls of wisdom and then
    He's led ruthlessly into the slaughter!

    A man provides meat and French beans for the table;
    He buys bonnets and laces and gloves.
    Then later he's asked to absorb the hard news
    That she's famished for wanting of love!

MYLES (*and any male musicians join in the chorus*):

    What is a man to do?
    Misguided and misinformed,
    He throws himself on the waters of life,
    And surrenders his dreams to the storm!

    A woman is proud, disordered, perplexing;
    A man strives to uncover the light.
    But all that he's learned from his father denies
    The disasterous forces of night.

    What is a man to do?
    Misguided and misinformed,
    He throws himself on the waters of life,
    And surrenders his dreams to the storm!

If there is to be an act break, it should be here, announced by SNAKE:

INTERMISSION

In Which the Audience Goes into a Different Space
and Talks about What It's All Meant to Mean

SCENE 10

In Which Ann First Puts on the Masks

ANN *is running in place, hunting for* SNAKE.

ANN: Snake! Snake! Help me! I need your help! Someone, please, anyone, Snake, help me!

Finally she falls down, exhausted.

SNAKE (*coming to her, pats her on the head*): Come on, kid. Buck up! It's not as bad as all that.
ANN (*looking up*): It is bad, Snake. It is as bad as all that. Something is really wrong with me. I don't know what to do.
SNAKE: Well, since you asked, I'll tell you what I think. As I see it, you've got four alternatives. Number one: You could bury yourself in the closet until the screaming meemies crawl out of your skin and drive everyone into the asylum. Two: You could get the hell out of the house and run until you find some other crazy game to fit into. Three: You could beat the shit out of those two women and kick *them* out of the house. Personally it's the one I favor, but then, I gotta admit I have a certain natural attraction for blood and violence. Or, four: You could take the masks they gave you for a wedding present and give them a whirl. Prediction: In the end it'll be a bust.

ANN: The masks! Of course! Why didn't I think of them?

ANN hunts down the masks and tries them on one at a time, getting more and more into playing CARLA and VERA, parading around in them.

SNAKE (*sings before the altar of the Terrible Goddess of the Blood-Seed*):

> Take the bone-wreath, Ann!
> Claim your anger,
> Own the life-consuming need,
> And listen to the call
> Of the Terrible Goddess
> Of the Blood-Seed!
>
> Take the bone-wreath, daughter!
> Face your madness,
> Dare the unrepenting deed,
> And listen to the call
> Of the Terrible Goddess
> Of the Blood-Seed!

MYLES (*enters*): Ann! Ann! There you are. I've been looking for you.
ANN (*behind VERA's mask, snuggles up to him*): Hi, Myles. You look worried.
MYLES: I am worried, Honey. 'Bout you. Haven't you noticed?
ANN: Don't you worry 'bout me, Myles. I feel happy as a little bird today.
MYLES: You do?
ANN: I do. Really, Myles. Things'll be different now. You'll see.

MYLES looks at ANN. She laughs. He laughs. Then they laugh together. They kiss.

MYLES: Where's Carla? What's for dinner?
ANN (*switching to CARLA's mask*): Dinner's on me.
MYLES: Huh?
ANN: I said: Dinner's on me tonight, Myles.
MYLES: You made dinner?
ANN: What's-a-matter? Cotton in your ears? Sit down. Eat. (*She serves him soup.*) I'm gonna be a good wife to you, Myles. I'm gonna do it right.

She stands behind him, placing her hand on his shoulder. He takes her hand, caresses it. She drops the mask momentarily, staring out at the audience.

SNAKE, DAD, VERA, CARLA, MUSICIANS (*any or all of them sing*):

> Powerful is the wish to give kisses freely.
> Powerful, too, the wish to have kisses returned.

Women are taught by their mothers and sisters before them
That no price is too high where the love of a man is concerned.

SCENE 11

In Which Myles Loses His Keys and Ann Finds Them

ANN *peers around the kitchen in* CARLA's *mask. She discovers* MYLES' *keys under the table. She sits on the table holding them and waits for* MYLES *to enter.*

ANN: Lose something, Myles?
MYLES: Hi, Honey! I didn't see you sitting there.
ANN: I asked you, did you lose something?
MYLES: My heart . . . to you.
ANN: Ha, ha, ha.
MYLES: What're you doin' with Carla's mask? Put it down . . . . Give a kiss.
ANN: You didn't answer my question.
MYLES: What question?
ANN: Did you lose . . . .
MYLES: Oh, yeh! Did I lose something. Besides my heart?
ANN: Get serious, Myles.
MYLES: Hmmmm. Okay. Serious. Got my cigarettes, got my shoes, got my jacket, got me k . . . . Oh, my God! My keys! They're gone Ann! My keys are gone! I can't do without them! I've lost them!

ANN *dangles the keys in front of his nose.* MYLES *looks somewhat mortified.*

MYLES: You found them.
ANN: It was nothing. Nothing at all, Myles. I'll watch out for you. I like taking care of you.
MYLES (*taking the keys*): Thanks, Ann.
ANN: Carla.
MYLES: What?
ANN: Carla. I like that name. I'd like you to call me Carla today.
MYLES: That's a stupid idea!
ANN: Who found your keys?

MYLES: You did.
ANN (*laughing good-naturedly*): Better not call me stupid.
MYLES: Okay. Okay, Ann.
ANN: Carla.
MYLES: What?
ANN: Call me Carla.
MYLES: Jesus Christ, Ann . . .
ANN: Carla!
MYLES: Okay! Carla! Carla, Carla, Carla! What's for dinner . . . Carla?
ANN: Soup.
MYLES: Again?
ANN: It's what we always eat. You like it. Or did you forget?
MYLES: You're flipping out. You really are flipping out.
ANN: Who keeps forgetting things? Who lost his keys?
MYLES: I merely mislaid them, Ann, momentarily.
ANN: Carla!!
MYLES: Carla!!
ANN (*ruffles his hair affectionately*): It's a good thing some of us still have our heads on straight. (*She dishes him up some soup.*) Eat.
SNAKE (*reading*): From the journal:

> VERA *peers over her shoulder, listening.*

> I am in a large meadow. I am a young girl. There is another girl there. She is very beautiful. She is my friend. She says to me: "We will play a game. We will be Amazons and we will kill all the Virgins and the Old Crones because they're not Amazons. They're the enemy." We sneak into the house on our hands and knees. Vera and Carla are in the kitchen. We leap up behind them and throw heavy ropes around their feet and their hands, throwing them down on the floor. We pull their clothes off them and lay burning matches on their skin. Then we poke out their eyes with forks. We cut off their fingers and make them suck on the blood. We laugh and dance around them, whooping and hollering as loud as we can. It's a wonderful game.

VERA: I knew it! Carla! Carla! I told you she was crazy! She's gonna try and kill us, Carla.
CARLA (*coming on and grabbing* VERA *by the arm*): Hush! Vera, hush! Just be quiet now and watch and see what happens. It's not gonna do us any good for you to go crazy, too!

SCENE 12

In Which Dad and Myles Have a Man-to-Man Talk

MYLES *and* DAD *come into the kitchen together.*

During this scene, ANN *paints a huge tear on the portrait of her mother.*

MYLES: Wine?
DAD: With pleasure . . . Myles. To the betterment of life!
MYLES: Skol!

They drink. Pause.

DAD: I gather from your letter, Myles, that you are harboring some doubts concerning the state of Ann's health.
MYLES: Yeh, Dad. I'm worried about her.
DAD: What appears to be the problem?
MYLES: She's been acting kind of funny, Dad. She just sits around all day, sulking. She always seems so sad. She doesn't say much about what's bothering her. And lately she's been wearing those masks . . . .
DAD: Masks?
MYLES: Yeh . . . Vera's and Carla's masks they gave her for a wedding present. She puts them on and pretends she's them.
DAD: Sounds like a harmless enough game. She might learn something, after all, Myles, about becoming a woman, a process it appears both Carla and Vera know a little more about than does Ann.
MYLES: I suppose so, Dad . . . . (*He drinks.*) Still . . . she's so sad all the time.
DAD: What about Carla? Can she help?
MYLES: Carla's fine.
DAD: Perhaps she could talk with Ann. A woman needs the companionship of other women, it being beyond our means to understand the moods and upheavals of the female cycle. They do not have the same intellectual grasp of their own internal mechanisms that we men do, you know.
MYLES: I'll talk to Carla, Dad. It's a good idea.

They drink. Pause.

MYLES: Whew! Marriage! I thought it would be easier.
DAD: Marriage is a consummation of difficult and perhaps debatable merit, a futile attempt to create a haven from the undiscriminating storms of life's routine labors, a perhaps unrealistic, unpragmatic, and idyllic flaunting of the universal laws of disillusionment and unequivocal despair, which con-

tains even in its preliminary fantasies an inevitable failure given the certainty of death!

Pause.

MYLES: How come you got married, Dad?
DAD: Sometimes it passes through my mind that the reason I married Ann's mother was that I was better than she and could prove a necessary and important component to her growth, could make her over, in a manner of speaking, save her from the trials of an otherwise unenlightened and pedestrian existence; and hence garner the satisfaction of having contributed to the bettering of the human race. When she died at an unpredictably early age, I transferred this rather unlikely pursuit to my daughter.
MYLES: Do you feel like you did it? I mean saved Ann from the trials of whatever you said?
DAD: I believe that I pursued my course with constant vigilance and dedication, instructing Ann in the Arts of Life and Love to the best of my knowledge. But there is a point beyond which it is impossible to ever reach or understand another person's soul. And it is that point which I seem to have reached, not only with Ann but (*he sighs*) with all women who have passed into and out of the boundaries of my humble care.
MYLES: You feel as helpless as I do . . . . Is that what you're saying, Dad?
DAD: Well, it is true that I am often beset now with a pressing feeling of futility. The dreams and the hopes are fading; the ice seems too thick to break. I feel myself turning sour, my intellectual and spiritual resources are drying up.
MYLES: You're a good man, Dad. I wish you'd talk simpler.
DAD: My soul needs watering.
MYLES: Have some more wine.

They drink.

DAD: It all raises a certain nostalgia which may in the end prove laughable.

They look at each other for a moment. They both laugh.

SNAKE, VERA, CARLA, MUSICIANS (*any or all of them sing*):

>   Perilous is the journey of the lover;
>   Perilous, too, a father's need to be strong.
>   Men are taught from their birth to slay their brothers.
>   Who will teach them the words to a different song?

Scene 13

In Which Myles Is Seduced by Ann

ANN *is wearing* VERA'S *mask. She has decked herself out with jewelry and high-heeled shoes.* MYLES *comes in.*

MYLES: Ann? Is that you?

ANN: Who'd you think? Vera perhaps? You're in love with Vera, aren't you, Myles?

She comes to him, humming something she thinks might be seductive. She moves from pose to pose, incongruously.

MYLES: Ann . . . ? You okay?

ANN (*dancing around, flaunting her body at* MYLES; *she seems crazed*):

> The Queen of Sheba went to a dance;
> But she forgot to wear her pants.
> All the king's horses and all the king's men
> Couldn't get Sheba to put her pants on again! . . . .

(*Peeking from behind the mask.*) Tut, tut, tut . . . Vera was always such a naughty child!

MYLES: Ann, I don't like it.

ANN: Like it? Like it, Myles? You're not supposed to like it! You should love it! Loathe it! Embrace it! Torment it! Eat it!

MYLES: Where's Carla?

ANN: How should I know?

MYLES: She should be here. She promised to watch you.

ANN: I sent her away.

MYLES: And Vera?

ANN: Gone, gone! They've all flown away, flown the coop! Lady bug, lady bug, fly away home; your house is on fire, your children will burn . . . . burn! Burn!

MYLES (*shaking her*): Where are Carla and Vera?

ANN (*stops what she is doing, drops the mask and looks him in the eye*): I don't know, Myles. Out. Out on a walk perhaps, buying clothes perhaps, planting carrots perhaps! Why always Vera and Carla, Carla and Vera? Why, Myles? Ann is here. (*She throws her head back, laughing, her mask back up.*) Happy to make your acquaintance. Shall we dance? (*She tries to engage him in her dance. She lowers the mask and winks at* MYLES. *He is won over.*)

MYLES (*laughing*): Okay, Ann, okay, okay.

He approaches her. She suddenly puts the mask back up, covering her face.

ANN: Game first.

MYLES: What game?

ANN: You know. Who do you love the most?

MYLES: Ann.

ANN: No, Myles. Vera. You love Vera the most. I like that name. I want you to call me Vera, Myles. I want you to call me Vera.

MYLES: Ann, I can't go through with this.

ANN: Not Ann, Vera. (*She caresses the word.*) Ve-ra, Ve-ra! It's been hard, hasn't it, Myles, me not giving you what you need . . . what any man needs . . . . Come on, Myles, say it: Vera . . . Vera . . . Vera. (*She rubs him seductively.*)

MYLES (*finally embracing her, laughing, kissing her*): Okay! Okay! Have it your way! Vera, vera, vera, vera, vera, vera, vera, vera, vera! Give us a kiss, Vera!!

As he begins to undress her, caressing her, without his noticing, she slowly lowers her mask and stares blankly out at the audience.

SNAKE/MOM (*reading, from behind her* MOM *mask*): From the journal: It is winter. Midnight. I am standing alone in front of our house. Suddenly a lion leaps out of the darkness at me. I get onto his back and he takes me down to the river. The river is packed with huge chunks of ice. The ice chunks change into skulls, hundreds of empty skulls, bumping into each other on the water's surface. They are white with age. They have been in the river for hundreds of years. I am surprised I never noticed them before. The lion takes me to a clearing where the lizard still lies in his tiny coffin. Beside his box is another one, much larger, made of the same crude wood. The lion indicates to me that I should get into this box. It is my coffin. I lie down in it and the sky opens up. Dirt comes pouring out of the sky. It covers me up. One eye is left open and I see the lion's mane bursting into flame. The fire climbs up into the sky, turning the whole universe into a red mist. I close my eye. I have reached the end of the road.

SCENE 14

In Which Vera and Carla Persuade Myles That Ann Is Crazy

VERA, CARLA, *and* MYLES *are standing in a row in the kitchen.* VERA *and* CARLA *have* MYLES *locked in a tight grip.*

SNAKE *is at the altar.*

CARLA: She's crazy, Myles!
VERA: She's flipped out. Lock her up!
CARLA: You'd better do something about it.
VERA: Get 'em to come for her.
CARLA: Seriously, Myles, she should be locked up.
VERA: She's looney!
CARLA: She's sick, Myles.
VERA: Nuts!
CARLA: But don't worry, Myles.
VERA: Don't worry. We'll be okay without her.
CARLA: You'll be okay. We'll take care of you.
VERA: We'll take care of you.
CARLA: We'll all be
VERA: Okay.
CARLA: You must
VERA: lock her
CARLA: up,
VERA: Myles!
CARLA: She's
VERA: nuts,
CARLA: Myles!
VERA: Flipped
CARLA: out! Lock
VERA: her
CARLA: up!
CARLA *and* VERA: Lock her up! Lock her up! Lock her up!
MYLES (*breaking away violently, he builds these "OKs" to express all his frustrations, anger, fear*): OK! OK! OK! OK! OK! OK! OK! OK! OK! OK!

ANN *brings her journal to* MYLES *to show him where to read while* SNAKE *sings. It is her last gift to him.*

SNAKE (*sings*):

> Take the bone-wreath, daughter!
> Face the madness,
> Dare the unrepenting deed,
> And listen to the call
> Of the Terrible Goddess
> Of the Blood-Seed

MYLES (*reading*): From the journal: I am a king. I sit on a huge gold throne. Beside me is another throne. It is empty. I know I must find the person who sits in this throne. I walk out of the palace. Beautiful women touch my face, some sing songs. They ask me to marry them. I brush them away. I come into the woods. It is very dark. The path ends and I am pushing through the briars. Suddenly I hear someone singing.

ANN (*sings from far away*):

> The rains come
> And the women cry
> And the waters rise
> And my love is a river of rage.

MYLES (*still reading*): I follow the voice until I come to a tiny clearing. Standing in the middle, singing up at the moon, is a girl. She is dressed in a long, brightly colored skirt, and she has a shawl around her arms. She isn't very pretty, but I know that I love her. I ask her to come back with me to the palace. She sees that I am lonely, and she comes. I let her sit on the throne next to mine. I give her jewels and perfumes. I bring bowls of strawberries to her and fresh milk. But she is sad. She becomes more and more unhappy. She stops singing. She is pale. She won't eat. I think: She is going to die. Finally I take her back to the woods. She puts her head on my chest for a moment and then she leaves. I come back to the palace. I sit on my throne alone. I cry. I cry for a very long time. I think: Perhaps I will never stop crying.

Scene 15

In Which Ann Has a Talk with Mom

ANN *begins quietly calling out for her mother. She builds her call into an eerie and primal scream: "Mama!"*

SNAKE *appears before her in some magical way like a Deus ex Machina. She is wearing* MOM'S *mask.*

SNAKE/MOM: Hiya, Honey!

ANN *looks up frightened.*

SNAKE/MOM: You called me, didn't ya?
ANN: Who are you?
SNAKE/MOM: You know who I am, Annie. You called for me.
ANN (*stamping her foot petulantly*): I thought you'd never come! You're late.
SNAKE/MOM: Well, my hearin's not so good now.
ANN (*swiftly, all the words running together*): Mom . . . I've been so bad. Oh, I don't want to be bad. I've been so bad. Myles has gone away. I mean he hasn't gone away. He's at the end of the water. I mean . . . I'm not making any sense. Am I making any sense?
SNAKE/MOM: Sure, Annie.
ANN (*brightening, skips around, holding her skirt and singing; suddenly she screams*): Mama!! I don't know what to do.
SNAKE/MOM: Sit down, Annie. (*Pause.*) Sit down beside me and I'll tell you a story. (*She hums a lullaby while* ANN *curls up with her head in* MOM'S *lap like a child.*) Once upon a time there was a little girl, and she had two wicked stepsisters . . . .
ANN (*interrupting*): Named Vera and Carla!
SNAKE/MOM: Yes. Named Vera and Carla.
ANN: And they were very very bad to the little girl and so one night she crept into their bedroom when they were asleep, and put a burlap bag over Carla's head (*she acts it out*) and chopped off Vera's hands, yes, and then her feet, oh, and the blood spurted out all over the rug and the walls and bed, and the sheets got all bloody. Then she cut off both their ear lobes and their noses, and then their feet, and their nipples! Oh! (*She is laughing.*) It was horrible. (SNAKE/MOM *laughs delightedly like a child.*) It was wonderful! (*Suddenly she looks at* SNAKE/MOM *in terror, realizing what she exposed.*) Oh! It's awful! (SNAKE/MOM *nods in agreement.* ANN *starts talking very fast.*) Mom, I wouldn't know what to do without Vera and

Carla. I wouldn't know how to take care of Myles; or how to keep him, Mom. He'd leave me. I'm sure he'd leave me if anything ever happened to Vera and Carla, Mom. I don't want that, no, I don't want him to go. Nothing can happen to Vera and Carla, Mom. Nothing. (*Pause.*) Is anything going to happen to them?

SNAKE/MOM: They're not real, Annie.

ANN: What?

SNAKE/MOM: They're made up. They don't really exist at all.

Pause.

ANN: Myles mustn't go. Mom, Myles mustn't leave me.

Pause.

Is he going to leave me? Is he? Is he going to leave?

SNAKE/MOM: I don't know.

ANN: I don't want to be all alone.

SNAKE/MOM: I know, Honey, I know.

ANN: Vera and Carla always . . . . Vera and Carla always take care of things. They'll take care of me.

SNAKE/MOM: They're not real, Annie. You made them up. Just like I did before you and just like all the women did and still do who live in a world ruled by men. (*Pause.*) 'Cause it's the only way we know how to survive. But they're not real, Annie. And you don't have to live with them if you don't want to.

Long pause. SNAKE/MOM *gets up to leave.*

ANN: You're not going, are you?

SNAKE/MOM: Yes, Annie. I am going.

ANN: You'll come back, won't you?

SNAKE/MOM: You won't need me, Annie.

She takes the mask off and reveals herself as SNAKE. *She gives the mask to* ANN *who fits it to her own face exactly, it being her own life mask.* SNAKE *leaves.*

Scene 16

In Which Ann Tries Unsuccessfully to Persuade Vera and Carla to Leave

ANN *is chasing* VERA *and* CARLA *around the kitchen with the ax.*

ANN: Get out! Get out!

CARLA: Annie! Annie! Put it down!

VERA: She's gone crazy, Carla! What did I tell you? It's that book done it! Made her go stark, raving mad! She's gonna kill us, Carla! She's gonna kill us!

CARLA: Now, Vera, you be still. Annie, listen to me. You don't want to hurt us, we're your sisters.

ANN: Just get out of here. Yes, I'd like to kill you, Vera, and you, too, Carla. Get out of here before I do!

VERA: What did I tell you?

ANN *comes after her.* VERA *screams. They chase around the table.*

CARLA: Now calm down, Ann.

ANN: I will not calm down until you get out of here. For good!

VERA: Where would we go?

CARLA: Shut up, Vera! She doesn't mean it.

MYLES (*enters*): Ann! Carla! What's going on?

VERA: Oh, thank God! It's Myles. (*She collapses against him.*)

MYLES (*grabbing the ax from* ANN *and holding on to her arm, to* VERA *and* CARLA): Sit down! Now — what in Hell's going on here?

VERA: She's flipped out!

CARLA: It's true, Myles. She's gone beyond the beyonds. She needs help.

ANN: I am simply asking them to leave my house.

VERA: "My house!" Get that! Who does she think she is? It's our house, too.

MYLES: Vera!

CARLA: Hush now, Vera.

VERA: Well, it is.

MYLES: No one is saying it isn't.

ANN: I am. I'm saying it isn't.

MYLES: Ann, Ann, these are your sisters.

ANN: They are not my sisters.

MYLES: These are your sisters, Ann, and they live here and they help us take care of the house and we love them and we couldn't get along without them, Ann. Now, what is it really?

VERA: She's crazy, Myles! She can't listen to reason! Lock her up!
CARLA: It's true, Myles. She needs help.
MYLES: What do you want, Ann?

Pause.

ANN: I don't know, Myles. I don't know what I want.

Silence.

CARLA: Well! I'm shaking like a leaf. I'm going to go lie down for a bit. She needs help, Myles. Call me if you need me. (*She exits.*)
VERA: I can't make any sense of it. What about you Myles? (*She rubs against him. He brushes her aside.* VERA *stares at* ANN *fixedly, hate in her eyes, and then exits.*)

Silence.

MYLES: I can't help you, Ann. I can't help you.
ANN: I know. I'll do it alone.

Each cast member whispers in turn, echoing ANN: *"I'll do it alone." And each turns her/his back on* ANN. *She slowly walks down to her journal.*

SNAKE, DAD, VERA, CARLA, MYLES, MUSICIANS (*sing*):

> Fabulous is the anger of the daughter;
> Fabulous, too, the terror of the son.
> Arduous is the long march into the center
> When darkness prevails and shadows cover the sun.

ANN (*reading from the journal*): I am standing on the edge of a very high cliff. The sky is a blue sweep of light. It is so bright, it presses into my eyes. I feel the earth moving under my feet. The cliff is breaking off. It is falling into the sea, falling. Dirt, grass, shrubs, falling. Down and down . . . into the sea. And I am standing here where the cliff used to be. I am standing on the air . . . effortlessly . . . .

She lets the book slip out of her hands onto the ground. ANN *stands in a single spot of light. For a very long time she stands there.*

SCENE 17

In Which Ann Burns the Masks

SNAKE *sets up this ritual. It is like a High Mass performed before the Terrible Goddess of the Blood-Seed. She has performed it many times before. There is a constant chanting under the scene, low and droning, by the others.*

SNAKE: How's it goin', kid?
ANN: I feel awful.
SNAKE: I can believe it — you look awful! Buck up! (*She slaps her on the back.* ANN *cries.*)
ANN: I feel sad.
SNAKE: Sad! You've been sad for four thousand years! Old Lady Sad-Sack! Maybe you oughtta try something else for a change.
ANN: For instance?
SNAKE: For instance, pissed! (*She gives a loud thwack with the ax on the chopping block.*) Let's begin.

SNAKE *lays* VERA's *and* CLARA's *masks in front of* ANN. *She moves the candle nearer to her, lights it and the others.*

Burn the goddamned masks, Ann!

SNAKE *shares bread and/or wine. She moves up to and around the altar, lighting the candles, offering the bread and wine, performing the centuries-old ritual.* SNAKE *muttering to herself while performing the ritual tasks.*

What are times coming to? Burn the masks, Ann. Chintzy candles. Used to have red ones. Now all we get's the girl scout variety. On good days at that. Prices and blood pressure. Ha! They always rise when the revolution begins. Halleluja! (*All echo low: "Halleluja!"*) No more free bones at the butchers. Now Ann. No heat left in the temples. No soup left in the pots. Burn them, Ann. No kerosene for the lamps. No glass for the windows. How will people see out? Ha. They'll have to see in. Burn them, Ann. Times are hard. getting harder. Praise the mother.

ANN *takes the masks and burns them in the candle flame. As she does so she sings plaintively. The song grows into a kind of a wail, unaccompanied.*

SNAKE *watches.*

ANN (*sings*):

> My love is a river;
> My love is a river of rage.
> Love rages through me,
> Love rages through me,
> Cracking the ice.
>
>> The rains come
>> And the women cry
>> And the waters rise
>> And my love is a river of rage.
>
> I lean on the shore
> And gather the seed.
> I carry the seed,
> I carry the seed
> On the back of the river.
> My love is a river;
> My love is a river of rage.

When ANN *is finished,* SNAKE *comes to her.*

SNAKE (*sings*):

> Take back the blood-seed;
> Lay down the bone-wreath;
> Take back your own.
> Bury the seed-corn
> Under the ground,
> Under the ground, Annie,
> Under the ground.

ANN (*sings*):

> Rain's comin',
> Ducks are flyin',
> New seeds got to be planted.

SNAKE *and* ANN (*sing together; the song becomes a celebration with everyone joining as the chorus builds*):

> New seeds got to be planted,
> Under the ground, Annie,
> Under the ground.

At the end ANN *is standing center on the table, where she remains for the rest of the play. She lifts the ax over her head.*

ANN *signals to* SNAKE *to usher* CARLA *and* VERA *out through the theater. Their voices carry off into the distance. There is a music which continues throughout.* ANN *watches.*

VERA: You'll be sorry for this, Annie!
CARLA: We could have helped you.
VERA: We're your sisters. You'll be sorry!
CARLA: We're on your side, Ann. Some day you'll regret this. (*Etc., ad lib.*)

There is a long silence. ANN *lowers her ax.* MYLES *enters.*

ANN: Myles?
MYLES: They've gone.
ANN: Yes. They've gone.
MYLES: You did it?
ANN: I did it.
MYLES: Now what?
ANN: We go on.
MYLES: You and me?
ANN: You go on. I go on. We move into the center of our own dreams.
MYLES: I dreamt I stood under a tree and all its leaves were gone. But the summer hadn't ended. It was terrifying.
ANN: I dreamt it, too.
MYLES: Where will you go?
ANN: I don't know, Myles.

MYLES *looks at* ANN *for a long time. She holds his gaze and then she finally turns to face the audience.*

I don't know.

MYLES *leaves.*

ANN: From the journal: I'm running beside the river. I'm running and running. I'm holding a bowl. It's made of red earth. It is cracked. Suddenly the moon falls out of the sky. I catch it in my bowl. It gives off a bright gold light. It is very beautiful. I come to the clearing. No one is there. I place my bowl in the center of the clearing at the side of the river. A hundred voices come out of the river. They are voices of women. The river is singing. The river is singing to me! I throw my journal into the river. Some of the songs are about me. They flow out of my journal. And there are hundreds of others. Songs about women — women's lives, women's dreams. The moon sits in my bowl. I listen all night to the river.

ALL (*sing*):

>The die is cast,
>The dead no longer singing.
>What's done is done.
>The pendulum is swinging.
>
>The question is laid out
>For each of us to ask:
>Whether to hold on
>Or to drop the mask.

The End

Love Song for an Amazon

THE CHARACTERS

Rose
Aisha, *pronounced* Ä-ē-ʹsha

This is a play for two women. It is a celebration and ritual enactment of their friendship — the multiple masks and the deep bonding. It is for you to provide the setting.

ROSE *and* AISHA *enter. They carry rocks, which they place in separate piles.*

BOTH: I feel.
How can I feel.
I feel.
I feel.
How can I feel?
I feel.
I feel feeling.
I feel dropping.
I feel how can I feel.
Feel.
Dropping.
Feeling.
I feel dropping.
Released.
I feel.
I feel.
I feel released.

AISHA *takes a rock from* ROSE*'s pile.*

ROSE: It isn't yours.
AISHA: You can't . . .
ROSE: Shame!
AISHA: Shame and can't.
ROSE: It isn't yours.
AISHA: It isn't nice.
ROSE: It isn't right.
AISHA: It isn't yours.
ROSE: Shame!
AISHA: And can't!
ROSE: Shame and can't.
AISHA: Shame and can't!

Pause.

ROSE: Once upon a time
there was a little girl.
There was a little girl.
And a window.
Once upon a time
there was a window.
AISHA: Don't go through the window.

>   Don't lean out the window!
>   Don't open the window!
>   Don't look out the window!

ROSE: Once upon a time
there was a little girl.
She had many dolls.
She had Rebecca and Dorothy
and Caroline and Cynthia
and Grey
and Cat
and Ozma
and Marianne and St. Theresa
and Jean and Dorothy and Rebecca.

Pause.

And Caroline.

Pause.

Every night she put them all to bed.
Every night she put them all to bed
before she put herself to bed.
She put herself to bed
and she dreamed the war.
She dreamed bombs.
She dreamed broken buildings.
She dreamed fire.
She dreamed screams.
She dreamed hiding under a blanket.
With huge holes to see out.
With huge holes
to see in.
She was not safe.

AISHA (*sings*):

    Robin sitting on a tree,
    You are there,
    And I am . . .

ROSE (*sings*):

    Robin sitting on a tree,
    You are there,
    And I am . . .

AISHA (*sings*):

          Robin sitting on a tree,
          You are there,
          And I am ...

ROSE (*sings*):

          Here.

Pause.

AISHA: What do you want?
ROSE: A chair.
    To sit on.
AISHA: You're just a child
    crying for the moon.

    ROSE *watches.*
    AISHA *rolls rocks across the floor at her.*

ROSE: She leaned over
    and she kissed me.
    She kissed me
    on the mouth.
    I held my breath.
BOTH (*breathe in swiftly, breathe out very slowly*):
    On the edge ... I stood on the edge ... not wanting to let go ... breathless ... breathless ... the sky was creaming ... white cream ... in the blood ... on the edge ... in the sky ... creaming ... creaming ... (*Pause.*) Hold my hand.

    Pause.

ROSE: It is well to understand that love ...
    It is well to understand that love is ...
AISHA (*whispers*): Too big to mention.

    Silence.
    ROSE *places the rocks in a row. She is testing* AISHA.

ROSE: Once upon a time a little girl —
AISHA: Cried all night long.
ROSE: Once upon a time a little girl —
AISHA: Ran all the way home.
ROSE: Once upon a time a little girl —
AISHA: Stole seven candy bars: five Almond Joys and two Mars Bars.
ROSE: Once upon a time a little girl —

AISHA: Imagined she had a sister.
ROSE: Where did she go?
AISHA: Where *did* she go?

Pause.

ROSE: Is this a play?
AISHA: No, this is a song.

She sings.

                    Wind.
                    Wind.
                    Wind.
                    Wind.

Pause.

You ought to be ashamed.
ROSE: You ought to be afraid.

Pause.

AISHA *throws the rocks chaotically.*

ROSE: Hey! What are you doing? What are you doing now?!

Silence.

AISHA: I'm prettier.
ROSE: I'm prettier.
AISHA: They all say I'm prettier.
ROSE: I'm cuter.
AISHA: I'm cuter.
ROSE: They all say I'm cuter.
AISHA: I'm smarter.
ROSE: Who cares?

Silence.

AISHA: At the bottom of the ocean
    there is a tiny shell.
    It hides among
    the sea anemones
    and the pink coral.
    It hides in the sand hills.
    It listens all day.
    It listens all day
    to the sea waves

>   singing.
>   It listens all day
>   to the people
>   talking.
>   It listens all day
>   to the singing
>   and the talking,
>   to the ranting
>   and the raving.
>   It never stops listening.
>   It has been listening
>   for a thousand
>   years.
>   It has been listening
>   to everything
>   that anyone
>   has ever
>   said.

ROSE: I'm going to find it.
AISHA: You're leaving?
ROSE: I'm going to find it.
AISHA: You said for always.
ROSE: I said for always for now.
AISHA: I knew it.
ROSE: Knew what?
AISHA: You'd leave.
ROSE: It doesn't matter.
AISHA: It does matter.
ROSE: Then come with me.
AISHA: I'd have an awful time.
ROSE: I'll go alone then.
AISHA: No.
ROSE: Is this a play?
AISHA (*sings*):

>   Wind.
>   Wind.
>   Wind.
>   Wind.

Pause.

ROSE: Quit it; stop; cease; can it; cut!

AISHA: Who are you?
ROSE: I'm the one who knows.
AISHA: The one who knows what?
ROSE: What they know.
AISHA: What do they know?
ROSE: What's best.
AISHA: What is best?
ROSE: What they know.
AISHA: Who?
ROSE: They.
AISHA: Who they?
ROSE: They they.
AISHA: What do they know?
ROSE: They know what's best.
AISHA: I know what's best.
ROSE: They know what's best.
AISHA: I know what's best.

Silence. AISHA *sits with the rocks in her lap.*

ROSE (*sings*):

> I had a friend
> And she sang me a song
> And the song said:
> Only you,
> Only you can know.
> And all night long I held her in my arms.

BOTH (*across the space, a ribbon of sound*):

> Never before such a holiness
> If I breathe I might break.
> Never before such a holy, holy holiness.

Silence.

AISHA: On the road . . .
ROSE: Women carrying sacks of rock.
AISHA: In the stores . . .
ROSE: Women carrying sacks of rock.
AISHA: In the schools . . .
ROSE: Women carrying sacks of rock.
AISHA: On the buses . . .
ROSE: Women carrying sacks of rock.

AISHA: In the theater . . .
ROSE: Women carrying sacks of rock.
AISHA: Where are they going?
ROSE: To build a temple.

Pause.

AISHA: Is this a play?
ROSE: This is a song.

Pause.

They lied.

Silence. They carry the stones to a new space and build a structure.

AISHA: I imagined.

Pause.

I saw.
By the fire's side,
I saw.
Your skin was
golden.
Your breasts,
golden.
By the fire's light
you lay naked
to me.
I massaged your body.
You were a warrior.

Pause.

And I was a warrior.
I had done this
many times before.
I rubbed the oil
between my palms.
I warmed the oil
between my palms.
I rubbed the oil
into your body.
Your skin was golden.
I massaged your body,
and you lay naked

to me.
I had done this
many times before.

Pause.

We lived with
other women.
Younger women, older
women,
dancers,
weavers,
midwives,
visionaries,
politicians.
I had done this
many times before.
Your breasts were golden.
By the fire's light,
your skin
was golden.
Your enormous strength was
familiar.
Nothing
was surprising.

Pause.

"What went wrong?" I asked.
"What went wrong?"

Pause.

You were a warrior.
I massaged
your body.
I warmed the oil
between my palms.
I rubbed the oil
into your body.
Your enormous strength
was not surprising.
"Did we fight among ourselves?" I asked.
"Did we caw and claw
and fight among ourselves?"

Pause.

The space was open.
There was an open space
for each of us
to walk in.
The love for one
was also the love
for another.
There was no difference.
ROSE: What went wrong?
AISHA: "What went wrong?" I asked.
There was space within.
The attack was from
outside.
ROSE: Barbarians!
AISHA: Invaders!
ROSE: From outside!
AISHA: We were contained.
We were too contained!

Pause.

We must reach them all.
ROSE: And be responsible to all.
AISHA: There are thousands now.
Returned.
ROSE: And new ones.
AISHA: We must reach them all.

Pause.

I rubbed the oil
into your body.
Your skin
was golden.
I remembered
I had done this
many times before.
Your breasts were
golden.

(*Pause.*)

It won't be long now,
sister.
It won't be long.
It won't be long.
BOTH (*sing*):
        It won't be long now, Sister,
        Won't be long, won't be long.
        It won't be long now, Sister,
        Won't be long.

The End

PLAYS BY MARTHA BOESING

Early Works

Accent on Fools (1957): One-act morality play, produced at Connecticut College for Women.

Ransom (1968): One-act transformation play for one woman and one man. Unproduced.

The Melting Cup (1968): Full-length play, sprung from a dream. Unproduced.

The Wanderer (1969-70): Commissioned and produced by the Minnesota Opera Company, based on the 56th Hexagram of the I Ching. Music by Paul Boesing.

Earth Song (1970): Commissioned and produced by the American Friends Service Committee for touring throughout New England and the Midwest. Music by Paul Boesing.

Earthquake (1971): Written in collaboration with Earth Family. Unproduced.

The Chameleons (1971): Songs and dialogs about marriage for one woman and one man. Music by Paul Boesing.

Shadows: A Dream Opera (1972-73): Based on seven dreams, written in collaboration with the Experimental Opera Company at the Academy Theater in Atlanta, Georgia. Music by Paul Boesing.

Journey to Canaan (1972-74): About the Israelites' forty-year trek through the desert, written in collaboration with the acting company at the Academy Theater for four women and four men. Music by Paul Boesing.

Recent Works

Pimp (1973): A short play about women selling each other out for men: a mother, her daughter whom she sells, and the wife of the buyer confront each other and themselves. Published in Rachel France, ed., *A Century of Plays by American Women* (New York: Richards-Rosen Press, 1978).

The Gelding (1975).

River Journal (1975).

Love Song for an Amazon (1976).

Mad Emma (1976): A tribute to Emma Goldman's passionate struggle for all oppressed peoples; for one woman, one young girl, and one man. Music by Paul Boesing.

The Moon Tree (1977): A full-length play about the four wives of a modern Bluebeard and their revolutionary struggle to name and celebrate their lunacy. For one man and five women.

Trespasso (1977): A short play for two women wrestling with the issue of control.

The Story of a Mother (1978): A full-length play for five women (written in collaboration with the women At the Foot of the Mountain) about the myths, the masks, and the true feelings which exist in the relationship between mothers and daughters; it evolves into a ritual event with the audience. Music by Roberta Carlson.

Photos by Gerry Zeck

I love the drawings in this book, partly because it was in doing them that I got to know the women At the Foot of the Mountain, and also because by doing them I kept myself alive in some ways during a time when I otherwise often felt lost. In these drawings I found a sense of strength and clarity. Martha's work evokes a lot of images in me and I began to trust this intuitive process of visualization. It's very exciting.

I'm working now as a muralist in the Minneapolis CETA program and am interested more and more in public and political visual art forms.

Leslie Bowman